BIBLE
PRAYERS
for all your needs

BIBLE
PRAYERS
for all your needs

by
CLIFT & KATHLEEN
RICHARDS

Victory House, Inc.
Tulsa, Oklahoma

Unless otherwise indicated, all Scripture quotations are taken from the *King James Version* of the Bible.

Scripture quotations marked NIV are taken from the New International Version. Those passages are taken from the HOLY BIBLE: NEW INTERNATIONAL VERSION © 1978 by the New York International Bible Society, used by permission of Zondervan Bible Publishers.

Scripture quotations marked NKJV are taken from *The New King James Version.* Copyright © 1958, 1987 by The Lockman Foundation, La Habra, California. Used by permission.

Prayers are paraphrased from these versions unless otherwise stated.

Bible Prayers for All Your Needs
Copyright © 1999 by
K. & C. International, Inc.
ISBN 0-932081-67-3 (Mass-market Paperback)

Published by Victory House, Inc.
P.O. Box 700238
Tulsa, Oklahoma 74170
(918) 747-5009
victoryhouse.net
victoryhousepublishers.com

CONTENTS

Introduction

But my God shall supply all your need according to his riches in glory by Christ Jesus. (Phil. 4:19)

God always answers believing prayer that is based upon the promises of His Word. His promises form the foundation of our faith, enabling us to reach out and receive all the Father has in store for us, as Peter points out, "According as his divine power hath given unto us all things that pertain unto life and godliness, through the knowledge of him that hath called us to glory and virtue: Whereby are given unto us exceeding great and precious promises: that by these ye might be partakers of the divine nature, having escaped the corruption that is in the world through lust" (2 Pet. 1:3-4).

The discovery of God's promises is like the discovery of a buried treasure. It fills our hearts with the kind of excitement that comes from anticipated blessings. The Bible assures us that God wants to meet every need we have, and the topical prayers of this book enable us to meditate upon God's promises, believe them, receive them, and pray them. When we turn God's promises into personal prayers, we begin to understand more fully and deeply how much God loves us and wants to bless us.

The only prerequisites are: knowing, believing, and accepting that God has personal promises for every need of our lives. *Bible Prayers for All Your Needs* addresses many of the common needs we share as human beings: emotional needs, physical needs, family needs, financial needs, and spiritual needs. Spiritual needs are important because we believe that when these needs are met, many of our other needs will be fulfilled as well. This understanding is based on the following promise from Jesus' heart: "But seek ye first the kingdom of God, and his righteousness; and all these things shall be added unto you" (Matt. 6:33).

Remember, as you read and pray, that the multitude of God's promises is our rightful inheritance as children of the King. We are princes and princesses in His royal family. As we learn what His promises are, believing and receiving them, dynamic faith is unleashed in our hearts, and we are transformed from being ineffectual doubters into strong believers who truly take our stand upon the promises of God's Word.

The truth is, as the prayers in this book reveal, God has already met all of our needs in Christ Jesus. Listen to the truth of His Word: "Blessed be the God and Father of our Lord Jesus Christ, who hath blessed us with all spiritual blessings in heavenly places in Christ" (Eph. 1:3). The Bible says that He has *already* blessed us with *every* spiritual blessing. Isn't this truth fantastic?

God, our loving Father, *wants* to meet our needs, *promises* to meet our needs, and *already has* met our needs through Christ Jesus and the Holy Bible — a book of promises from God's heart to ours. He has called us to glory and virtue, and He has supplied us with all that we need to attain this godly goal. His great and precious promises are the means by which we participate in His divine nature and escape the corruption of the world. (See 2 Pet. 1:3-4.)

Each promise in God's Word is a need-meeting promise — a personal gift from God the Father to His children whom He loves with an everlasting love. In His Word, our Father tells us that His covenant with us is eternal, and every promise that stems from His covenant with us is for us to claim and activate in our lives.

God promises much more to us than most people realize. He has declared, "Eye has not seen, nor ear heard, nor have entered into the heart of man the things which God has prepared for those who love Him — but God has revealed them to us through His Spirit" (1 Cor. 2:9-10, NKJV).

God's promises are life and they are victory. They are spiritual stepping-stones to abundant living in the here-and-now. When you pray the prayers of this book, each of which is built directly from the promises of God, you will be able to realize His answers for each of your needs even as you pray, because you will be praying God's will for you. The Bible says, "And this is the confidence that we have in him, that, if we ask any thing according to his will, he heareth us: And if we know that he hear us, whatsoever we ask, we know that we have the petitions that we desired of him" (1 John 5:14-15).

To pray according to God's will is to pray according to His Word. Therefore, we cannot go wrong when we pray God's promises, because they are His revealed will for us. Each promise directly meets a human need.

For all the promises of God in him are yea, and in him Amen, unto the glory of God by us. Now he which stablisheth us with you in Christ, and hath anointed us, is God; Who hath also sealed us, and given the earnest of the Spirit in our hearts. (2 Cor. 1:20-22)

This Book of the Law shall not depart from your mouth, but you shall meditate in it day and night, that you may observe to do according to all that is written in it. For then you will make your way prosperous, and then you will have good success. (Josh. 1:8, NKJV)

The prayers of this book put you in touch with the heart of God. They will change your perspective, your attitudes, and your circumstances, because they reveal all that God has in store for you. Truly, they will meet your every need as they remind you of God's great love for you. They will build your faith to enable you to reach out and receive the fulfillment of all your needs.

Be blessed as you read and pray.

1

◆

THE BOOK OF ALL BOOKS BY THE KING OF ALL KINGS

1

The Book of All Books by the King of All Kings

The Bible Is a Safe That Holds Your Deed of Inheritance

The Bible is the Book of books because it was inspired by the King of kings. It sets forth the rules, regulations, and responsibilities that apply to each member of the Kingdom. It is also a book that is filled with promises from the King to His family. In fact, the Word of God is your deed of inheritance to all that God has put in reserve for you.

Your Father has left you with an incredibly rich inheritance in the form of a never-depleted trust fund. You are entitled to draw from that fund at any time in order to meet any need. To discover all the wonderful riches you've inherited, simply turn to His Word:

> *And now, brethren, I commend you to God, and to the word of his grace, which is able to build you up, and to give you an inheritance among all which are sanctified. (Acts 20:32)*

> *The Spirit itself beareth witness with our spirit, that we are the children of God: And if children, then heirs; heirs of God, and joint-heirs with Christ; if so be that we suffer*

with him, that we may be also glorified together. (Rom. 8:16-17)

And if ye be Christ's, then are ye Abraham's seed, and heirs according to the promise. (Gal. 3:29)

Eye hath not seen, nor ear heard, neither have entered into the heart of man, the things which God hath prepared for them that love him. (1 Cor. 2:9)

And whatsoever ye do, do it heartily, as to the Lord, and not unto men; Knowing that of the Lord ye shall receive the reward of the inheritance: for ye serve the Lord Christ. (Col. 3:23-24)

Faith is the key that opens the safe to all that God has for you. The safe is contained within His holy Word. Abraham Lincoln wrote, "In regard to this great book, I have but to say, it is the best gift God has given to man. All the good Savior gave to the world was communicated through this book. But for it we could not know right from wrong. All things most desirable for man's welfare, here and hereafter, are to be found portrayed in it."

The Bible Is Your Infallible Authority

Bible Prayers for All Your Needs reveals how the Bible is an ultimate source of authority for your life. As you pray the truths of the Word, spiritual authority is unleashed in your life.

By praying the promises, you are incorporating God's truth into every area of your life. Many amazing things happen when people learn to pray the promises of God. Our faith grows. Our attitudes change. Our hearts are softened. We transcend our problems. Our point of view becomes more congruent with God's perspective. Daily miracles take place. We achieve victory over our problems. And this is only a partial list of the blessings to be derived from praying God's promises.

Let God's Word be your ultimate authority as you pray His promises:

> *All scripture is given by inspiration of God, and is profitable for doctrine, for reproof, for correction, for instruction in righteousness. (2 Tim. 3:16)*

> *Every word of God is pure: he is a shield unto them that put their trust in him. (Prov. 30:5)*

> *So shall my word be that goeth forth out of my mouth: it shall not return unto me void, but it shall accomplish that which I please, and it shall prosper in the thing whereto I sent it. (Isa. 55:11)*

> *For all the promises of God in him*
> *are yea, and in him Amen, unto the*
> *glory of God by us. (2 Cor. 1:20)*

All God's promises are for you. When you pray His promises, His automatic answer is, "Yes!" God cannot violate His own will. What He promises, He fulfills.

John Locke wrote, "The Bible is one of the greatest blessings bestowed by God on the children of men. It has God for its author, salvation for its end, and truth without any mixture for its matter. It is all pure, all sincere; nothing too much; nothing wanting."

The Bible is alive because it is the Book of the Living God. His authority is documented on every page, and He wants us to share in its life.

The Bible Is a Guidebook for Daily Life

The Bible is translatable into daily living. The Psalmist wrote, "Thy word is a lamp unto my feet, and a light unto my path" (Ps. 119:105). We need to go to the Bible regularly, open it prayerfully, read it (and pray it) expectantly, and live it joyfully.

Bible Prayers for All Your Needs is a great companion in your study of the Scriptures, because it is a personal guide to a life of prayer that is based on the unfailing promises of God. It is also an open door to a spiritual adventure that knows no limitations as you apply its approach to your prayer life. We invite you to walk through that open door and discover all God has in store for you as you learn how to pray God's promises by knowing, believing, receiving, and living the Word of God.

> *When thou goest, it shall lead thee; when thou sleepest, it shall keep thee; and when thou awakest, it shall talk with thee. For the commandment is a lamp; and the law is light; and reproofs of instruction are the way of life. (Prov. 6:22-23)*

> *Then said Jesus to those Jews which believed on him, if ye continue in my word, then are ye my disciples indeed; And ye shall know the truth, and the truth shall make you free. (John 8:31-32)*

> *I will instruct thee and teach thee in the way which thou shalt go: I will guide thee with mine eye. (Ps. 32:8)*

> *And thine ears shall hear a word behind thee, saying, This is the way, walk ye in it, when ye turn to the right hand, and when ye turn to the left. (Isa. 30:21)*

> *As he spake by the mouth of his holy prophets, which have been since the world began. . . . To give light to them that sit in darkness and in the shadow of death, to guide our feet into the way of peace. (Luke 1:70-79)*

Johann Goethe wrote, "It is a belief in the Bible, the fruits of deep meditation, which has served me as the guide of my moral and literary life. I have found it a capital safely invested, and richly productive of interest."

Immanuel Kant echoes Goethe's sentiments in the following quote: "The existence of the Bible, as a book for the people, is the greatest benefit which the human race has ever experienced. Every attempt to belittle it is a crime against humanity."

The Bible Is a Rock of Strength

When we stand upon the solid rock of God's Word, nothing shall ever prevail against us. John Greenleaf Whittier puts it well, "We come back laden from our quest, To find that all the sages said, Is in the Book our mothers read."

Matthew Arnold concurs with Whittier when he writes, "To the Bible men will return, and why? Because they cannot do without it."

We need the promises of God's Word. This is one of the heart's deepest needs.

> *Heaven and earth shall pass away, but my words shall not pass away. (Matt. 24:35)*

> *For ever, O Lord, thy word is settled in heaven. (Ps. 119:89)*

> *The grass withereth, the flower fadeth: but the word of our God shall stand for ever. (Isa. 40:8)*

> *Blessed be the Lord, that hath given rest unto his people Israel, according to all that he promised: there hath not failed one word of all his good promise. (1 Kings 8:56)*

> *For I am the Lord: I will speak, and the word that I shall speak shall come to pass; it shall be no more prolonged. (Ezek. 12:25)*

> *He brought me up also out of an horrible pit, out of the miry clay, and set my feet upon a rock, and established my goings. (Ps. 40:2)*

The Bible has the power to stabilize your life. It is a permanent rock of refuge for every believer.

Find Strength in the
Promises of God's Word

The Psalmist prayed, "My soul melteth for heaviness: strengthen thou me according unto thy word" (Ps. 119:28). God's Word gives strength to your soul and body.

There is no book like the Bible, because there is no other book that has the power of God's promises at work on every page. Receive His strength as you meditate upon His promises:

> *For thus saith the Lord God, the Holy One of Israel; In returning and rest shall ye be saved; in quietness and in confidence shall be your strength. (Isa. 30:15)*

> *That he would grant you, according to the riches of his glory, to be strengthened with might by his Spirit in the inner man; That Christ may dwell in your hearts by faith; that ye, being rooted and grounded in love,*

> *May be able to comprehend with all saints what is the breadth, and length, and depth, and height;*

> *And to know the love of Christ, which passeth knowledge, that ye might be filled with all the fulness of God. (Eph. 3:16-19)*

President Woodrow Wilson wrote, "When you have read the Bible, you will know that it is the Word of God, because you will have found it the key to your own heart, your own happiness, and your own duty."

In short, the Bible will meet your every need as you learn to accept its truth, obey its commands, and pray its promises. The Word of God is your greatest need because it has the power to meet your every need.

2

◆

PRAYER, AND THE PROMISES
OF GOD

Prayer, and the Promises of God

But we will give ourselves continually to prayer, and to the ministry of the word. (Acts 6:4)

The Fulfillment of Your Needs

God has given us several promises in His Word that pertain directly to prayer. From these, we learn that it is clearly His will for us to pray. This is the way He has chosen to meet our needs. In fact, He calls us to prayer: "Call to Me, and I will answer you, and show you great and mighty things, which you do not know" (Jer. 33:3, NKJV). God never tires of hearing His people pray, and He never tires of meeting our needs. Isn't it wonderful that our Father in heaven wants to reveal great and mighty things to us?

The great Apostle Paul asked the Ephesians to pray for him because he clearly recognized the need-meeting power of prayer: "And [pray] for me, that utterance may be given unto me, that I may open my mouth boldly, to make known the mystery of the gospel, for which I am an ambassador in bonds: that therein I may speak boldly, as I ought to speak" (Eph. 6:19-20). Amazing spiritual power and authority, Paul recognized, are unleashed in response to intercessory prayer.

Paul knew the power of prayer. Repeatedly, he urged others to: "Pray for us" (1 Thess. 5:25), and "Finally, brethren, pray for us, that the word of the Lord may have free course, and be glorified, even as it is with you" (2 Thess. 3:1).

Surely it was the power of God, unleashed through intercessory prayer, that met Paul's needs in so many adverse circumstances of his life: "Are they ministers of Christ? (I speak as a fool) I am more; in labours more abundant, in stripes above measure, in prisons more frequent, in deaths oft. Of the Jews five times received I forty stripes save one. Thrice was I beaten with rods, once was I stoned, thrice I suffered shipwreck, a night and a day I have been in the deep; In journeyings often, in perils of waters, in perils of robbers, in perils by mine own countrymen, in perils by the heathen, in perils in the city, in perils in the wilderness, in perils in the sea, in perils among false brethren; In weariness and painfulness, in watchings often, in hunger and thirst, in fastings often, in cold and nakedness . . . " (2 Cor. 11:23-27). Yes, Paul knew the power of prayer which had seen him through each of those dilemmas, and he knew the power of God's promises to meet his every need.

Prayer Promises of Health and Healing

God wants to meet your physical needs.

Prayer produces both physical and spiritual power in our lives. The Bible is filled with examples that show the direct correlation between prayer and healing in several instances.

> *Then Peter said, Silver and gold have I none; but such as I have give I thee: In the name of Jesus Christ of Nazareth rise up and walk. (Acts 3:6)*

Through prayer, a man who had been lame from birth was healed. Prayer has the power to bring God's promises of healing to the afflicted.

> *And the prayer of faith shall save the sick, and the Lord shall raise him up; and if he have committed sins, they shall be forgiven him. (James 5:15)*

> *And he said unto him, Arise, go thy way: thy faith hath made thee whole. (Luke 17:19)*

The Word-faith-prayer connection must not be overlooked, because it is so vitally important when we are praying for our own needs or the needs of others. The Word of God produces the faith we need in our hearts to enable us to receive God's answers. (See Rom. 10:17.) When we pray in faith, believing God's promises, we receive them. The leper in Luke 17:19 learned this all-important connection when he placed his faith in Jesus as the Great Physician. James affirms this when he tells us that it is the prayer of faith that will save the sick.

Other prayer promises related to healing are given below:

> *And the king answered and said unto the man of God, Intreat now the face of the Lord thy God, and pray for me, that my hand may be restored me again. And the man of God besought the Lord, and the king's hand was restored him again, and became as it was before. (1 Kings 13:6)*

> *O Lord my God, I cried unto thee, and thou hast healed me. (Ps. 30:2)*

> *He sent his word, and healed them, and delivered them from their destructions. (Ps. 107:20)*

> *There came also a multitude out of the cities round about unto Jerusalem, bringing sick folks, and them which were vexed with unclean spirits: and they were healed every one. (Acts 5:16)*

> *But Peter put them all forth, and
> kneeled down, and prayed; and turning
> him to the body said, Tabitha, arise.
> And she opened her eyes: and when she
> saw Peter, she sat up. And he gave her
> his hand, and lifted her up, and when
> he had called the saints and widows,
> presented her alive. And it was known
> throughout all Joppa; and many
> believed in the Lord. (Acts 9:40-42)*

Bible Prayers for All Your Needs contains
Bible prayers for healing and health, based
upon the promises of God. They are not
magical formulas, but they are faith-building
meditations that enable the person in need to
reach out for all God has for them.

When King Hezekiah became terminally
ill, the Prophet Isaiah came to him and
prophesied, "Thus saith the Lord, Set thine
house in order; for thou shalt die, and not
live" (2 Kings 20:1).

Hezekiah responded with prayer: "I
beseech thee, O Lord, remember now how I
have walked before thee in truth and with a
perfect heart, and have done that which is
good in thy sight" (2 Kings 20:3). Then the
king began to weep.

The Lord gave a new word to Isaiah:
"Turn again, and tell Hezekiah the captain of

my people, Thus saith the Lord, the God of David thy father. I have heard thy prayer. I have seen thy tears: behold, I will heal thee" (2 Kings 20:5).

The Lord has given this example of God's healing power to show how promise-packed prayer, expressed in heart-felt faith, meets our physical needs. Yes, God does hear our prayers, and He promises, "If thou wilt diligently hearken to the voice of the Lord thy God, and wilt do that which is right in his sight, and wilt give ear to his commandments, and keep all his statutes, I will put none of these diseases upon thee, which I have brought upon the Egyptians: for I am the Lord that healeth thee" (Exod. 15:26).

Prayer Promises of Prosperity

God wants to meet your financial needs as well. One of the most stirring Bible passages related to prosperity is found in the Book of Deuteronomy. This passage is filled with personal promises for each of us to claim:

Blessed shall be thy basket and thy store. Blessed shalt thou be when thou comest in, and blessed shalt thou be when thou goest out. The Lord shall cause thine enemies that rise up against thee to be smitten before thy face: they

shall come out against thee one way,
and flee before thee seven ways. The
Lord shall command the blessing upon
thee in thy storehouses, and in all that
thou settest thine hand unto; and he
shall bless thee in the land which the
Lord thy God giveth thee. The Lord
shall establish thee an holy people unto
himself, as he hath sworn unto thee, if
thou shalt keep the commandments of
the Lord thy God, and walk in his
ways. And all people of the earth shall
see that thou art called by the name of
the Lord; and they shall be afraid of
thee. And the Lord shall make thee
plenteous in goods, in the fruit of thy
body, and in the fruit of thy cattle, and
in the fruit of thy ground, in the land
which the Lord sware unto thy fathers
to give thee. The Lord shall open unto
thee his good treasure, the heaven to
give the rain unto thy land in his
season, and to bless all the work of
thine hand: and thou shalt lend unto
many nations, and thou shalt not borrow.

And the Lord shall make thee the
head, and not the tail; and thou shalt be
above only, and thou shalt not be
beneath; if that thou hearken unto the
commandments of the Lord thy God,

which I command thee this day, to observe and do them:

And thou shalt not go aside from any of the words which I command thee this day, to the right hand, or to the left, to go after other gods to serve them. (Deut. 28:5-14)

What a powerful passage from the Scriptures this is. It is a promise of full prosperity and abundance for all who walk in the Lord's ways, and obey His commandments. More specifically, this passage promises that God will meet your needs by providing you with the following blessings:

1. Happiness.

2. A full measure of divine provision.

3. The blessing of the Lord wherever you go.

4. Protection from your enemies.

5. The Lord's blessings on all your possessions.

6. The Lord's blessings on your work.

7. The Lord's blessings on your land.

8. The blessing of being firmly established as the Lord's child.

9. Prosperity for your family.

10. Others will notice that you belong to the Lord.

11. The blessing of more than enough. (Abundance)

12. Prosperity that you can share with others.

13. No more need to borrow from others.

14. You will be the head, not the tail.

15. You will be on the top, not on the bottom.

These blessings are part of your rightful inheritance as a child of the King, and you are able to claim them (receive them) through faith and prayer.

Joshua gives us another divine promise of prosperity and blessing:

> *Only be thou strong and very courageous, that thou mayest observe to do according to all the law, which Moses my servant commanded thee . . . . This book of the law shall not depart out of thy mouth; but thou shalt meditate therein day and night, that thou mayest observe to do according to all that is written therein: for then thou shalt make thy way prosperous, and then thou shalt have good success. Have not I commanded thee? Be strong*

*and of a good courage; be not afraid,
neither be thou dismayed: for the Lord
thy God is with thee whithersoever
thou goest. (Josh. 1:7-9)*

Notice the connection Joshua makes
between adherence to the Word of God and
financial blessing. Praying the Scriptures is a
key to both prosperity and success when it is
mingled with courage and obedience.

Another case in point concerns Job who
learned that when he prayed for his friends,
with compassion and faith, God restored his
prosperity: "And the Lord turned the captivity
of Job, when he prayed for his friends: also
the Lord gave Job twice as much as he had
before" (Job 42:10). The prayer-faith-obedience
connection is a three-fold cord that pulls our
needs to us, right from the Father's hands.

Sometimes when people experience
prosperity, they begin to forget the Lord. Not
so, however, with the Psalmist who said,
"And in my prosperity I said, I shall never be
moved" (Ps. 30:6). Then he prayed, as if to
give himself a reminder, "Lord, by thy favour
thou hast made my mountain to stand strong:
thou didst hide thy face, and I was troubled.
I cried to thee, O Lord; and unto the Lord I
made supplication" (Ps. 30:7-8).

The above passages are but a few of those which promise prosperity to the obedient believer. However, all the Bible verses on this subject clearly show that meditating on and praying God's promises, in faith, do bring prosperity to the believer. This is particularly emphasized in Psalms 1:

> *Blessed is the man who walks not in the counsel of the ungodly, nor stands in the path of sinners, nor sits in the seat of the scornful; But his delight is in the law of the Lord, and in His law he meditates day and night. He shall be like a tree planted by the rivers of water, that brings forth its fruit in its season, whose leaf also shall not wither; and whatever he does shall prosper. (Ps. 1:1-3, NKJV)*

It is our privilege, as children of the King, to walk in the blessings of prosperity. Praying God's promises brings these blessings into our lives. When we pray God's promises He determines to meet our every financial need.

Prayer Promises of Revival

God promises to meet your need of personal, spiritual revival, and He promises to bring revival to hearts, homes, and churches around the world in response to Bible-based prayers of intercession. We're seeing answers to these prayers daily. Jesus said, "The harvest truly is plenteous, but the labourers are few; Pray ye therefore the Lord of the harvest, that he will send forth labourers into his harvest" (Matt. 9:37-38).

God promises, "If my people, which are called by my name, shall humble themselves, and pray, and seek my face, and turn from their wicked ways; then will I hear from heaven, and will forgive their sin, and will heal their land" (2 Chron. 7:14). God wants to bring revival, but the prerequisites for Him doing so are humility, prayer, seeking the Lord's face, and repentance among His people.

The Psalmist prayed, "Wilt thou not revive us again: that thy people may rejoice in thee?" (Ps. 85:6).

Likewise, Habakkuk the prophet prayed: "O Lord, I have heard thy speech, and was afraid: O Lord, revive thy work in the midst of the years, in the midst of the years make known; in wrath remember mercy" (Hab. 3:2). God heard and answered the prophet's prayer: "God came from Teman, and the Holy One from mount Paran. Selah. His glory covered the heavens, and the earth was full of his praise" (Hab. 3:3).

Collective revival begins with personal revival, and one key to personal revival is found in praying the promises, as the Psalmist did so often. He prayed, "Restore unto me the joy of thy salvation; and uphold me with thy free spirit. Then will I teach transgressors thy ways; and sinners shall be converted unto thee" (Ps. 51:12-13).

A prayer of the Psalmist that is found in Psalms 119 is particularly meaningful today: "It is time for thee, Lord, to work: for they have made void thy law" (Ps. 119:126). In prayer, the Psalmist is claiming God's promise of revival.

God wants to meet your need for revival, and He wants to meet the world's need for revival as well.

Prayer Promises of Direction

God wants to meet your need for direction and guidance.

Throughout the Scriptures God promises to guide and direct His people. We claim His promises of direction through prayer.

Based on the truths of the Word of God, we can pray with the Psalmist: "Lead me, O Lord, in thy righteousness because of mine enemies; make thy way straight before my face" (Ps. 5:8). The Lord wants to lead us when we are willing to follow His direction.

"He leadeth me beside the still waters" (Ps. 23:2).

"Lead me in thy truth, and teach me: for thou art the God of my salvation; on thee do I wait all the day" (Ps. 25:5).

"The meek will he guide in judgment: and the meek will he teach his way" (Ps. 25:9).

"He will be our guide even unto death" (Ps. 48:14).

"And the Lord shall guide thee continually" (Isa. 58:11).

"Thou shalt guide me with thy counsel" (Ps. 73:24).

God wants us to personalize each of these promises when we are seeking guidance and direction for our own lives. An appropriate Bible-based prayer at such a time would be: "Heavenly Father, you have promised to be my Guide until I die. Lead me and guide me continually. Guide me with your counsel, and make your way straight in front of me. Lead me in your truth and teach me, for you are the God of my salvation. Father, I wait on you." Notice how we have personalized God's promises regarding guidance and direction by turning them into prayer.

This prayer is formed from a collage of God's promises related to His direction in our lives. No prayer for guidance and direction could be more valid, because this prayer is based upon the Word of God, which tells us that God wants to meet all our needs.

God will meet your need for guidance and direction at all times.

Prayer Promises of Victory

God has already met your need for victory, because He wants you to be a winner, not a loser. He wants you to be a victor, not a victim. He wants you to be on the top, not on the bottom. He wants you to be strong, not weak. He wants you to be the head, not the tail. And the beautiful part of all this is that He promises to supply your needs so that you will be a winner, a victor, and a person who is on the top, not on the bottom — an individual who is truly at the head of the crowd.

When the Psalmist found himself in the midst of trouble, he prayed God's promises: "Though I walk in the midst of trouble, thou wilt revive me: thou shalt stretch forth thine hand against the wrath of mine enemies, and thy right hand shall save me" (Ps. 138:7). The Psalmist believed God's promises and he used them as his prayer, fully expecting God to hear him, answer him, and give him victory.

This is effective praying, and it always brings results.

Isaiah prophesied God's promise of victory to us: "When you pass through the waters, I will be with you; And through the rivers, they shall not overflow you. When you walk through the fire, you shall not be burned, nor shall the flame scorch you" (Isa. 43:2, NKJV).

Because of these promises, which assure us of God's presence being with us, we never have to fear. "Who shall separate us from the love of Christ? Shall tribulation, or distress, or persecution, or famine, or nakedness, or peril, or sword? . . . Nay, in all these things we are more than conquerors through him that loved us" (Rom. 8:35-37).

God promises victory for you and yours.

Prayer Promises for Your Family

God wants to meet the needs of your family.

His Word contains wonderful promises for mothers, fathers, husbands, wives, and children. For example, we find this glistening promise in the Book of Acts: "Believe on the Lord Jesus Christ, and thou shalt be saved, and thy house" (Acts 16:31). What a source of reassurance this is for every family member who is concerned about the salvation of a loved one. This promise fulfills our need to know that our loved ones will be saved, if we will pray for them.

God speaks to parents: "Train up a child in the way he should go: and when he is old, he will not depart from it" (Prov. 22:6). Every parent has a need to know that their children will turn out okay, and God understands this need, so He gives each one a promise that cannot fail. When we pray for our children's future, therefore, we can know that God is at work behind the scenes in their lives.

To children, God promises: "Honour thy father and thy mother: that thy days may be long upon the land which the Lord thy God giveth thee" (Exod. 20:12). This is a powerful promise for children from our heavenly Father who points out that longevity is associated with honoring one's parents.

The Word of God admonishes husbands to: ". . . love your wives, even as Christ also loved the church, and gave himself for it" (Eph. 5:25). This is such practical advice, for love that is given out is usually returned to us. There is, as well, a blessing to be derived from loving, for loving is its own reward.

The wife of an obedient man, the Bible promises, ". . . shall be as a fruitful vine by the sides of thine house: thy children like olive plants round about thy table" (Ps. 128:3).

At least one prayer promise draws a close connection between a healthy husband-and-wife relationship and getting one's prayers answered: "Likewise, ye husbands, dwell with them according to knowledge, giving honour unto the wife, as unto the weaker vessel, and as being heirs together of the grace of life; that your prayers be not hindered" (1 Pet. 3:7).

In the Kingdom of God, we're learning more and more, everything is connected. There is a mind-body-spirit connection, to be sure, and a direct connection between trustful obedience and obtaining God's promises. The Spirit and the Word are one in power. A husband and a wife are one in flesh. Jesus is the incarnate Word. Praying God's will is praying His Word. The Father, the Son, and the Holy Spirit are one. Believers are one in Christ.

When we pray for our families from this perspective, we realize that all these powerful forces are united in our behalf.

God wants to meet the needs of your family.

Prayer Promises of Emotional Health

God promises to bless you emotionally.

The promise-prayers of this book lead you to understand how God wants to move in your behalf when you are discouraged, worried, lonely, depressed, confused, tempted, angry, or guilty. As you pray the promises of God, you learn that God is always there to lead you into greater realms of emotional health and security.

Through the promises, you are able to see that emotions are not your lord, and circumstances are not your master. The One who is your Lord and Master desires to bless you with a greater portion of love, faith, hope, confidence, happiness, security, and joy. As you pray, you will find your fear turned into faith, your despair turned into hope, and your worry turned into peace.

Let the promises of His Word lift you up:

I can do all things through Christ which strengtheneth me. (Phil. 4:13)

And all things, whatsoever ye shall ask in prayer, believing, ye shall receive. (Matt. 21:22)

The Lord is my helper, and I will not fear what man shall do unto me. (Heb. 13:6)

Though I walk in the midst of trouble, thou wilt revive me: thou shalt stretch forth thine hand against the wrath of mine enemies, and thy right hand shall save me. (Ps. 138:7)

Let not your heart be troubled: ye believe in God, believe also in me. (John 14:1)

Be careful for nothing; but in every thing by prayer and supplication with thanksgiving let your requests be made known unto God. And the peace of God, which passeth all understanding, shall keep your hearts and minds through Christ Jesus. (Phil. 4:6-7)

Casting all your care upon him; for he careth for you. (1 Pet. 5:7)

Therefore the redeemed of the Lord shall return, and come with singing unto Zion; and everlasting joy shall be upon their head: they shall obtain gladness and joy; and sorrow and mourning shall flee away. (Isa. 51:11)

Because he hath set his love upon me, therefore will I deliver him: I will set him on high, because he hath known my name. He shall call upon me, and I will answer him: I will be with him in trouble; I will deliver him, and honour him. (Ps. 91:14-15)

Call unto me, and I will answer thee,
and shew thee great and mighty things,
which thou knowest not. (Jer. 33:3)

Oh, the rich promises of God's holy
Word. They are life and emotional health for
each of us. All we have to do is reach out in
faith and receive them. The result will be
unending joy.

Prayer Promises of Spiritual Growth

God wants you to grow in Him. He
promises, "The righteous shall flourish like
the palm tree: he shall grow like a cedar in
Lebanon" (Ps. 92:12). How does such growth
take place in our lives? The Lord answers
with another promise: "Let the word of
Christ dwell in you richly in all wisdom;
teaching and admonishing one another in
psalms and hymns and spiritual songs,
singing with grace in your hearts to the Lord"
(Col. 3:16).

The end result of learning, meditating
on, believing, receiving, and praying His
promises is declared in another Bible
promise: "That we henceforth be no more
children, tossed to and fro, and carried about
with every wind of doctrine, by the sleight of
men, and cunning craftiness, whereby they lie
in wait to deceive; But speaking the truth in

love, may grow up into him in all things, which is the head, even Christ" (Eph. 4:14-15).

Paul's advice to Timothy is good advice for every believer: "Meditate upon these things; give thyself wholly to them; that thy profiting may appear to all" (1 Tim. 4:15).

Bible Prayers for All Your Needs is written so that you will be: "Strengthened with all might, according to his glorious power, unto all patience and longsuffering with joyfulness" (Col. 1:11).

God promises to help you grow if you accept His promises and live in accord with them.

The Bible is your infallible authority for doing so, and praying the Word is an avenue to His blessings that is paved with the promises of God.

THE MOST IMPORTANT NEED

1. Salvation

Key Scripture: *"For by grace are ye saved through faith; and that not of yourselves: it is the gift of God: Not of works, lest any man should boast" (Eph. 2:8-9).*

Key Thought: You must be born again. (See John 3:3.)

Prayer: Precious Father, thank you for sending your love to me in the form of Jesus Christ, who died for me to save me from my sin.[1] You commended your love to me, O God, by letting Jesus die for me even while I was yet a sinner.[2] Such wonderful love truly amazes me.

According to your holy Scriptures, Christ died for my sins, was buried, and rose again the third day.[3] Thank you for your Word, Father, and for the living Word — Jesus Christ.[4]

Your Word of faith is near me, and it is in my mouth. With my mouth, Lord God, I confess that you raised Jesus Christ from the dead. Thank you for saving me as I believe in Jesus and your Word with all my heart, and I confess that He has saved me from my sins.[5] Thank you for so great a salvation.[6]

Father, I realize that I am a sinner, and I have fallen far short of your glory.[7] I also realize that my sin has earned me the wages of death, but how I thank you for the gift you've given to me — eternal life through Jesus Christ, my Lord.[8] Thank you for giving me eternal life with you, Father, in your Son, my Savior, Jesus Christ.[9]

Because I have Jesus, I know I now have life. Thank you, Lord God. I believe on the name of Jesus Christ, and now I know I have eternal life.[10] I receive Jesus Christ as my Savior and Lord, and I rejoice in the realization that you have given me the power to become your child.[11]

By your grace, through faith, I am saved. Thank you for your gift of salvation.[12] Hallelujah!

References: *(1) John 3:16; (2) Romans 5:8; (3) 1 Corinthians 15:3-4; (4) John 1:1-5; (5) Romans 10:8-10; (6) Hebrews 2:3; (7) Romans 3:23; (8) Romans 6:23; (9) 1 John 5:11; (10) 1 John 5:12-13; (11) John 1:12.*

SPIRITUAL NEEDS

1. Abiding in Christ

Key Scripture: *"And now, little children, abide in him; that, when he shall appear, we may have confidence, and not be ashamed before him at his coming" (1 John 2:28).*

Key Thought: Abiding means to be vitally united.

Prayer: Heavenly Father, I seek to abide in Christ. I realize that this is the key to fruitfulness in my life. Jesus is the Vine, and I am a branch. I need to continually abide in Him, for without Him I can do nothing.[1]

I will abide in Jesus, and I will let His words abide in me. I thank you for your promise, Father, that this will enable me to ask what I will, knowing that it shall be done.[2] Thank you for your Word[3] which helps me to always pray according to your will.[4]

Father, with all my heart, I desire to keep your Word. Perfect your love in my life so that I will constantly abide in Jesus, and learn to walk as He walked, and to love as He loved.[5] With your help, I will follow His example and walk in His steps.[6]

I pray now, Father-God, asking you, according to the riches of your glory, to strengthen me with might by your Spirit in my innermost being so that Christ may fully dwell and abide in my heart by faith, and so that I may be rooted and grounded in love.[7]

Thank you for the blessings of abiding in Christ.

References: *(1) John 15:4-5; (2) John 15:7; (3) 2 Timothy 3:16; (4) 1 John 5:14-15; (5) 1 John 2:3-6; (6) 1 Peter 2:21; (7) Ephesians 3:16-17.*

2. Ministry of Angels

Key Scripture: *"For he shall give his angels charge over thee, to keep thee in all thy ways. They shall bear thee up in their hands, lest thou dash thy foot against a stone" (Ps. 91:11-12).*

Key Thought: Angels are God's messengers and my protectors.

Prayer: Heavenly Father, thank you for the ministry of angels in my life. It gives me great comfort to realize that you have given them charge over me in order to keep me at all times.[1] I praise you for angels, O God.

Thank you, Father, for sending angels (your ministering spirits) to minister to all believers.[2] I believe and receive their ministry in my life. Give me a greater appreciation and understanding of the work of angels in my life, O God. I realize there are thousands of angels, and I thank you that you are in their midst.[3]

Thank you, Father, that hundreds of thousands of angels are ministering to you,[4] and I thank you that you allow your angels to minister to me in so many ways.[5] Thank you for my guardian angels that continually behold your face in heaven.[6]

It gives me great comfort and a wonderful sense of security to realize that your angels are encamping around me, and to know that they are always ready to deliver me.[7] In the same way that you sent the angel to shut the lion's mouth in order to protect Daniel,[8] I ask you to let your angels watch over and protect me.

Thank you, Father, for the power of Jesus Christ in my life. He is the brightness of your glory and the express image of your person, and He upholds all things by the word of His power. Thank you for the fact that He has purged me of all my sins, and now sits at your right hand. The inheritance He has received permits Him to obtain a more excellent name than even the name of angels. I join with the angels of heaven, Lord God, in honoring Jesus Christ, because I know that through Him, you have made your angels a flame of fire in my life.[9]

Thank you for angels, Father.

References: (1) Psalms 91:11; (2) Hebrews 1:14; (3) Psalms 68:17; (4) Daniel 7:9-10; (5) Hebrews 1:7; (6) Matthew 18:10; (7) Psalms 34:7; (8) Daniel 6:22; (9) Hebrews 1:3-7.

3. When You Doubt Your Salvation

Key Scripture: *"He that hath the Son hath life; and he that hath not the Son of God hath not life"* (1 John 5:12).

Key Thought: Assurance of salvation comes by faith.

Prayer: Heavenly Father, I rejoice in and thank you for all the promises of your Word which proclaim that I can know for sure that I am born again and I am going to heaven. Because I have confessed with my mouth the Lord Jesus, and have believed in my heart that you raised Him from the dead, I know I am saved.[1] It's no longer a matter of wishing so, thinking so, or hoping so, because it is a matter of knowing so. Thank you, Father.

I have heard your Word and I have believed in Jesus Christ. Now I have everlasting life, and I shall not come into condemnation. You have brought me from death to life.[2] Thank you, Lord God. By your grace I have been saved, not through my own efforts at all. Thank you for your gift of salvation.[3]

I am now crucified with Christ. Nevertheless, I live; yet it is not I who lives, but Christ who lives within me. And the life I now live in the flesh I live by the faith of the Son of God, who loved me, and gave himself for me.[4] By faith in Christ Jesus, Father, I have become your child.[5] Thank you for adopting me into your family.[6]

Now that I know that I am saved, beyond all shadow of doubt, I will fight the good fight of faith, lay hold on eternal life to which you have called me, and profess a good profession before all.[7] I will hold fast the profession of my faith without wavering, because I know you are faithful with all your promises.[8]

Thank you for enabling me to be born again, dear Father.[9]

References: (1) Romans 10:8-9; (2) Romans 8:2; (3) Romans 6:23; (4) Galatians 2:20; (5) John 1:12; (6) Galatians 4:5; (7) 1 Timothy 6:12; (8) Hebrews 10:23; (9) John 3:5-8.

4. Freedom From Bitterness

Key Scripture: *"Let all bitterness, and wrath, and anger, and clamour, and evil speaking, be put away from you, with all malice" (Eph. 4:31).*

Key Thought: The opposite of bitterness is sweetness.

Prayer: Help me, mighty Father, to keep the attitudes of my heart, the thoughts of my mind, and the words of my mouth free from bitterness at all times. When either circumstances or other people's actions try me, may I be like Hannah who responded with prayer when she was experiencing bitterness of soul.[1] She prayed to you, weeping profusely, and you heard and answered the cry of her heart. You turned her bitterness into joy.[2]

My heart is heavy with my own bitterness.[3] Knowing that you know more about me than I do, I choose to obey you by not spending my years in the bitterness of my soul.[4] Restore me, and make me live. Grant me your peace, and deliver my soul from the pit of corruption. Thank you, wonderful God, for casting all my sins behind your back.[5]

I repent of the sin of bitterness in my life, fully realizing that it has defiled me and others.[6] From this time forward, I will forsake all bitterness, wrath, anger, quarreling, resentment, and evil speaking. I put them behind me now.

I will not allow these things to be a part of my life any longer. In their place, I will be kind, tender-hearted, and forgiving toward others even as you, dear God, have forgiven me.[7]

References: (1) *1 Samuel 1:10; (2) 1 Samuel 1:20; (3) Proverbs 14:10; (4) Isaiah 38:15; (5) Isaiah 38:16-17; (6) Hebrews 12:15; (7) Ephesians 4:31-32.*

5. Knowing the Power of Jesus' Blood

Key Scripture: *"In whom we have redemption through his blood, the forgiveness of sins, according to the riches of his grace" (Eph. 1:7).*

Key Thought: There is wonder-working power in the blood of Jesus.

Prayer: Heavenly Father, thank you for the blood of Jesus which, through your eternal Spirit, purges my conscience from dead works in order to enable me to serve you.[1] Thank you for redeeming me through the precious blood of Christ who became an eternal sacrifice for my sins, without any blemishes or imperfections.[2] Through your Son, Jesus Christ, who shed His blood for me, I am able to believe in you, Father, because your Word assures me that you raised Jesus from the dead and gave Him glory so that all my faith and hope would be in you.[3]

Through the blood of Jesus you have reconciled me to yourself, Father, and being reconciled, I am likewise saved through His life.[4] Thank you so much for the power of His blood. Your Word shows how the Israelites applied sacrificial blood to the doorposts of their houses in order to keep the plague from coming near their dwellings.[5] I claim the protective power of Jesus' blood for me and my family, Lord. I praise you for your promise that assures me that when you see the blood of Christ, you will be sure to protect us.[6] Thank you, Father.

You teach me in your Word that I am able to overcome the enemy, Satan, by the blood of the Lamb, and by the word of my testimony.[7] Therefore, I plead the protection of the blood of Jesus Christ over my home and family, and I know you will plant your hedge of protection around us,[8] because, as for me and my house, we will serve you.[9]

Help me, Father, to walk in the light as Jesus is in the light, because I know this will enable me to have true fellowship with other believers, and the blood of Jesus Christ will cleanse me from all sin.[10] The blood of Jesus was shed for the remission (forgiveness) of my sins.[11] Therefore, I know I am freely justified by His grace through the redemption His blood provides for me.[12]

Thank you, Father, for sending Jesus to be a sacrifice for my sins, and I respond to this fact of my faith with total trust in the power of His blood. With your help, I will declare His righteousness to the world, and I will accept the certainty that all my sins have been fully remitted through His blood.[13] In the same way that I have been justified through His blood, I know I will be saved from wrath through Him.[14]

Father, thank you for the power of Jesus' blood in my life.

References: (1) Hebrews 9:14; (2) 1 Peter 1:18-19; (3) 1 Peter 1:20-21; (4) Romans 5:10; (5) Exodus 12:13; (6) Exodus 12:13; (7) Revelation 12:11; (8) Job 1:10; (9) Joshua 24:15; (10) 1 John 1:7; (11) Matthew 26:28; (12) Romans 3:24; (13) Romans 3:25; (14) Romans 5:9.

6. When You Need Greater Faith

Key Scripture: *"Above all, taking the shield of faith, wherewith ye shall be able to quench all the fiery darts of the wicked" (Eph. 6:16).*

Key Thought: Reading God's Word imparts faith to our hearts. (See Rom. 10:17.)

Prayer: Your Word, Father, renews my mind so that I am able to prove what your good, acceptable, and perfect will in my life is.[1] Your wonderful Word also imparts faith to my heart.[2] Thank you, Lord.

Through your grace, I will wash in the cleansing, sanctifying waters of your Word every day.[3] The truth of your Word sanctifies me.[4] Thank you, Father.

Your Word helps to increase my faith because its power is at work in my life. Thank you for the life-giving power of your Word, Father.[5] I rejoice in the knowledge that you are changing me from glory to glory by your Spirit.[6] As I meditate upon the principles of your Word, my faith grows and I am blessed.[7]

Realizing, Father, that it is impossible to please you without faith, I come to you fully believing in you and knowing that you will reward me because I am diligently seeking you.[8] Thank you for enabling me to have faith in you and your Word. The faith you've imparted to me is the substance of things I hope for, and it is the evidence of things I do not yet see.[9] Thank you, Father. I realize that the things that are seen are temporal and subject to change, but the things that are not seen are eternal.[10]

Through faith I am able to understand so many things, including the fact that the very worlds of the universe were framed by your Word. This helps me to understand that things which are seen were not made of things which I can see. Instead, they were made by your unseen hand, O Lord.[11] Therefore, I will walk by faith and not by sight.[12]

Through faith, you enable me to subdue kingdoms, work the works of righteousness, obtain all of your promises, and even stop the mouths of lions.[13] Through faith I shall be able to quench the violence of fire, escape the edge of the sword, turn my weaknesses into strengths, become valiant in all struggles, and turn my enemies away.[14]   Thank you for increasing my faith, Father, through your Word.

References: *(1) Romans 12:2; (2) Romans 10:17; (3) Ephesians 5:26; (4) John 17:17; (5) Hebrews 4:12; (6) 2 Corinthians 3:18; (7) Psalms 1; (8) Hebrews 11:6; (9) Hebrews 11:1; (10) 2 Corinthians 4:18; (11) Hebrews 11:3; (12) 2 Corinthians 5:7; (13) Hebrews 11:33; (14) Hebrews 11:34.*

7. Walking in Faithfulness

Key Scripture: *"A faithful man shall abound with blessings: but he that maketh haste to be rich shall not be innocent"* (Prov. 28:20).

Key Thought: Faithfulness in our lives stems from being full of faith.

Prayer: Dear God, thank you for the fruit of faithfulness.[1] I desire to always be faithful in every area of my life. I yield myself to the work and power of your Holy Spirit, who enables me to walk in faithfulness by being steadfast, unmoveable, trustworthy, and to be always abounding in your work, O God.[2]

Great is your faithfulness, O God,[3] and I draw near to you now with a true heart, in full assurance of faith, having my heart sprinkled and purified from an evil conscience by the blood of Christ. It is this truth that enables me to hold fast the profession of my faith without wavering, knowing that you are always faithful to your promises.[4]

I praise you, Father, that you are at work in me, both to will and to do your good pleasure.[5] I believe you are producing the fruit of faithfulness in my life because I know this is your will for me. Thank you for helping me to be faithful and true.

References: (1) Galatians 5:22; (2) 1 Corinthians 15:58; (3) Lamentations 3:23; (4) Hebrews 10:22-23; (5) Philippians 2:13.

8. Spiritual Freedom

Key Scripture: *"And ye shall know the truth, and the truth shall make you free" (John 8:32).*

Key Thought: The people of God know perfect freedom.

Prayer: Lord God, thank you for your truth which makes me truly and completely free.[1] As your servant, I will walk in the amazing spiritual freedom and the glorious liberty you give to your children,[2] and I will stand fast in the liberty Christ has given to me, and I will never again be entangled with any yoke of bondage.[3]

Where your Spirit is, Lord, there is liberty,[4] and because this is true, I determine to walk in the Spirit each step of the way.[5] As I walk in the Spirit, the lusts of my flesh will not be fulfilled, and you will lead me.[6]

Thank you, Lord God, for calling me to freedom. I will use my wonderful spiritual freedom to serve others through love.[7] Your powerful Word is the law of liberty in my life, Lord, and I will continue to walk in your Word and in the perfect liberty it gives to me. With your help, I will be a doer of your Word, Father-God, and not just a hearer.[8]

The power of your gospel and the Spirit of life in Christ Jesus have set me free from the law of sin and death.[9] Hallelujah, I'm free indeed of all sin, guilt, and fear. Thank you, Father.

O God, you have given me total spiritual freedom. Whereas once I was bruised and scarred by sin, I am now free, enjoying your healing and deliverance in every area of my life. Your Spirit is upon me, and you have anointed me to proclaim your gospel, to heal the broken-hearted, to minister your deliverance, and to give sight to the blind. Through the power of your Spirit, Lord, I will be able to lead others into freedom.[10]

Thank you for full spiritual freedom, my Lord and my God.

References: (1) John 8:32; (2) Romans 8:21; (3) Galatians 5:1; (4) 2 Corinthians 3:17; (5) Galatians 5:16; (6) Galatians 5:18; (7) Galatians 5:13; (8) James 1:25; (9) Romans 8:2; (10) Luke 4:18.

9. Walking in Gentleness

Key Scripture: *"But the fruit of the Spirit is love, joy, peace, longsuffering, gentleness, goodness, faith, meekness, temperance: against such there is no law" (Gal. 5:22-23).*

Key Thought: God's Spirit produces the fruit of gentleness in my life.

Prayer: God, you are gentle,[1] kind,[2] and plenteous in mercy.[3] Thank you for giving me gentleness as a fruit of your Spirit.[4]

As your servant, Lord, I will endeavor to walk in the fruit of gentleness toward all others. With your help, I will exhibit the qualities of gentleness, through patience, meekness, and kindness at all times.[5]

Show me how, Father, to be clothed with tender mercy, kindness, humility, meekness, patience, and forgiveness, so that I will walk in gentleness faithfully.[6] As I learn to walk in gentleness, O God, I will put on love which is the bond of perfection, and I will let your peace rule in my heart, and be thankful.[7] Your fruit of love is the source and foundation of all gentleness in my life.[8]

Therefore, I will let your Word dwell richly within me in all wisdom, gentleness, and truth.[9] With your help, Lord, I will do everything in the name of the Lord Jesus, giving thanks to you through Him.[10]

References: *(1) 2 Samuel 22:36; (2) 2 Samuel 2:6; (3) Psalms 86:5; (4) Galatians 5:22; (5) 2 Timothy 2:24-25; (6) Colossians 3:12-13; (7) Colossians 3:14-15; (8) Galatians 5:22; (9) Colossians 3:16; (10) Colossians 3:17.*

10. Giving God First Place

Key Scripture: *"I am Alpha and Omega, the beginning and the ending, saith the Lord, which is, and which was, and which is to come, the Almighty" (Rev. 1:8).*

Key Thought: You belong to God.

Prayer: Dear God, I realize I am not my own. I have been bought with a price — the price of the precious blood of Jesus.[1] I am crucified with Christ. Nevertheless, I live; yet it is not I, but it is Christ who lives within me. The life I now live in the flesh, I live by faith in the Son of God who loved me and gave himself for me.[2] I embrace your Word which tells me that I am dead to sin, and my life is hid with Christ in God.[3]

Because of your great love, I am risen with Christ, and I will seek those things which are above, where Christ sits at your right hand.[4] Father-God, I commit myself to giving you first place in my life at all times. I will seek first your kingdom, and your righteousness, and I thank you for taking care of me.[5]

Your Word declares that my heart will be found where my treasure is. Lord, I want you to be my treasure.[6] You are the one God, the Father of all, and you are my Father. You are above all and through all, and in all believers.[7] Help me, Father, to keep you first in my life, and to keep all the priorities of my life in line with yours.

Father, I am so honored to be your child, and I appreciate the presence of your Holy Spirit both with me and within me.[8] Lord, it thrills me to know that you have first place in my life in the here-and-now, and I rejoice to know that this will continue throughout all eternity, and we will be together forever.[9]

You are my love, you are my life, you are my breath, you are my all in all.

References: *(1) 1 Corinthians 6:20; (2) Galatians 2:20; (3) Colossians 3:3; (4) Colossians 3:1; (5) Matthew 6:33; (6) Matthew 6:21; (7) Ephesians 4:6; (8) John 14:17; (9) Revelation 19:6.*

11. Glorifying the Lord

Key Scripture: *"I will praise thee, O Lord my God, with all my heart: and I will glorify thy name for evermore" (Ps. 86:12).*

Key Thought: Glorifying God makes His presence more real.

Prayer: O God, I love to glorify you, and to praise your holy name. I will bless you at all times, and your praise shall continually be in my mouth,[1] for you are the King of all the earth.[2]

Yours, O Lord, is the greatness, and the power, and the glory, and the victory, and the majesty. For all that is in heaven and in the earth is yours. Yours is the kingdom, O Lord, and you are exalted as the head over all.[3] Now, therefore, my God, I thank you, and I praise your glorious name,[4] for you are good, and your mercy endures forever.[5]

Because your lovingkindness is better than life to me, my lips shall praise you, and I will bless and glorify you while I live. I will lift up my hands in your name. As you satisfy my soul as with marrow and fatness, my mouth will praise you with joyful lips.[6]

Holy, holy, holy, are you, Lord God almighty, which was, and is, and is to come.[7] You are worthy, O Lord, to receive glory and honor and power, for you have created all things, and for your pleasure they are and were created.[8]

References: *(1) Psalms 34:1; (2) Psalms 47:7; (3) 1 Chronicles 29:11; (4) 1 Chronicles 29:13; (5) Psalms 107:1; (6) Psalms 63:3-5; (7) Revelation 4:8; (8) Revelation 4:11.*

12. God's Faithfulness

Key Scripture: *"Thy mercy, O Lord, is in the heavens; and thy faithfulness reacheth unto the clouds" (Ps. 36:5).*

Key Thought: God is always there.

Prayer: Faithful Father, I know you are always there for me.[1] Thank you for calling me into fellowship with you through your Son.[2] Not one word of all your good promises has ever failed in my life,[3] and I know you will never leave me nor forsake me.[4] I rejoice in the certain knowledge, Father, that you are my very present help in times of need.[5]

Throughout my life I have never seen the righteous forsaken.[6] Even when I am lacking in faith, Father, you are always faithful to me.[7] I know you know me because I am yours.[8] You always hear my cry.[9] You know my ways.[10] You recognize my voice.[11] How I thank you that I am your servant and you always deal well with me.[12] Father, thank you for always being faithful to your Word.[13] It gives me great confidence to realize that your Word will never return to you empty, but it will always accomplish what you desire, and it will achieve the purposes you have in mind.[14]

You always have, and I know you always will, faithfully accomplish your purposes in my life.[15] I know you will keep me, Father.[16] Your Word never fails.[17] Thank you for letting me experience your great faithfulness in my heart and in my soul.[18] Thank you for loving me.[19] You are my faithful Father, and you always keep your covenant with me.[20]

You, my great and glorious Father, will never permit my foot to be moved. Thank you for never sleeping or slumbering as you watch out for me. I know you are watching out for me even now.[21] Thank you for always being there for me.[22] I rejoice in the knowledge that your mercy endures forever.[23]

References: *(1) 1 Corinthians 1:9; (2) 1 Corinthians 1:9; (3) 1 Kings 8:56; (4) Hebrews 13:5; (5) Psalms 46:1; (6) Psalms 37:25; (7) 2 Timothy 2:13; (8) 2 Timothy 2:19; (9) Psalms 28:1; (10) Psalms 1:6; (11) Psalms 141:1; (12) Psalms 119:65; (13) Psalms 119:65; (14) Isaiah 55:11; (15) 1 Thessalonians 5:24; (16) Genesis 28:15; (17) Joshua 23:14; (18) Joshua 23:14; (19) 1 John 4:19; (20) Deuteronomy 7:8-9; (21) Psalms 121:3-4; (22) Psalms 46:1; (23) Psalms 136:1.*

13. When You Need God's Forgiveness

Key Scripture: *"If we confess our sins, he is faithful and just to forgive us our sins, and to cleanse us from all unrighteousness" (1 John 1:9).*

Key Thought: God has forgiven you, is forgiving you, and will forgive you through your personal confession of sin.

Prayer: Heavenly Father, I thank you for forgiving me of my sins. As you promised, when I sin I do have an advocate with you — Jesus Christ, the Righteous One. He paid the penalty for all my sins.[1] Thank you for granting repentance to my heart, Father. I specifically repent of my sin(s) of: _____
_____. As I confess my sin to you, I turn my back on my sin and, with your help, I am determined to follow you and your ways at all times.

I realize, Lord, that it is by taking heed to your Word that I can keep myself from sin, and through your grace, this I will do. With my whole heart I will seek you; don't let me wander from your commandments. I have hidden your Word in my heart so that I might never again sin against you.[2]

Thank you, Father, that guilt no longer has any dominion in my life whatsoever. You have set me free from all guilt. Thank you for imparting your righteousness to me through

Jesus Christ who knew no sin. It was He who became sin for me so that I might be made righteous in you.[3] Thank you, Father.

Unto you, O Lord, I lift up my soul, for I know you are good, and you are always ready to forgive. You are plenteous in mercy unto all who call upon you.[4] I do so now, in the full assurance that your forgiveness is for me. Thank you, Father.

Thank you for forgiving me of my iniquities and for remembering them no more. Lord, you have removed my sins from me as far as the east is from the west.[5] Help me to be like you, Father, in that I never want to remember my sins ever again.[6]

Now I know I am forgiven. I am restored. Thank you for the power of your forgiveness in my life, Father.

References: *(1) 1 John 2:1-2; (2) Psalms 119:9-11; (3) 2 Corinthians 5:21; (4) Psalms 86:4-6; (5) Psalms 103:12; (6) Hebrews 8:12.*

14. The Fullness of God

Key Scripture: *"And to know the love of Christ, which passeth knowledge, that ye might be filled with all the fulness of God" (Eph. 3:19).*

Key Thought: Let's be filled with all the fullness of God.

Prayer: Dear God, I love you, and I desire to be filled with all your fullness. Therefore, I bow my knees to you, God, my Father, and the Father of my Lord Jesus Christ, of whom the whole family in heaven and in earth is named. Grant to me, according to the riches of your glory, that I would be strengthened with might by your Spirit in my innermost being.

Let Christ dwell in my heart by faith so that I, being rooted and grounded in your love, may be able to comprehend with all saints the breadth, length, depth and height of Christ's love. Father, enable me to know and experience fully the love of Christ, which surpasses human knowledge.

Fill me with all your fullness. Thank you for always being present with me.

Thank you, Father, that you are able to do exceedingly abundantly above all that I ask or think, according to your great power that is at work within me. Thank you, Lord.

Unto you, O God, be glory in the Church by Christ Jesus throughout all ages, world without end. Amen.[1]

References: *(1) Ephesians 3:14-21.*

15. When You Need to Know the Love of God

Key Scripture: *"Behold what manner of love the Father has bestowed on us, that we should be called children of God!" (1 John 3:1, NKJV).*

Key Thought: God loves you!

Prayer: Heavenly Father, thank you for loving the world so much that you gave your only begotten Son, that whosoever would believe in Him should not perish, but have everlasting life.[1] Truly, there is no greater love than yours, Lord.   Thank you for sending Jesus to redeem the world, and for saving me.

Help me, Father, to always remember that I am able to love only because you first loved me.[2]   Because you love me, you've given me commandments to follow, and because I love you, I want to obey you always.[3] Because you have saved me and made me a new creation in Christ, I can love others as you have loved me. Through this means, Lord, I know that others will realize that I am a disciple of Jesus Christ.[4]

Thank you for your perfect love which casts out all fear from my life.[5] Your amazing love shows me how to love sincerely, without any hypocrisy.[6] Thank you, Father.

I rejoice in the fact that there is no limit to your love, Lord. It is from everlasting to everlasting. You have poured your love abroad in my heart by the Holy Spirit who has been given to me.[7] Strengthen me with might by the Holy Spirit so that I will be able to comprehend with all saints the full extent of your love.[8]

Your Son, my Lord and Savior, Jesus Christ, dwells in my heart by faith, and I thank you that you are rooting and grounding me in His love. Above all else, Lord, I desire to know your love which passes knowledge and to be filled with all your fullness.[9]

Thank you for loving me, Father.

References: (1) John 3:16; (2) 1 John 4:19; (3) John 14:15; (4) John 13:34-35; (5) 1 John 4:18; (6) Romans 12:9; (7) Romans 5:5; (8) Ephesians 3:18-20; (9) Ephesians 3:19.

16. God's Protective Armor

Key Scripture: *"Put on the whole armour of God, that ye may be able to stand against the wiles of the devil" (Eph. 6:10-11).*

Key Thought: God's armor is impenetrable.

Prayer: Heavenly Father, I thank you for the armor you have provided for me to wear for protection from all assaults. Help me to remember to put on each piece of your armor carefully every day, and to never forget to dress myself in your protective gear. I will gird up my loins with your truth and put on the breastplate of righteousness. I will wear the shoes of the preparation of your gospel of peace, and I will buckle the shield of faith to my forearm. On my head, I will place the helmet of salvation as I take up the sword of your Spirit (your most precious Word). I will pray with all supplication in your Spirit, and I will faithfully watch thereunto with all perseverance and supplication for all saints.[1]

Give me insight into the cunning craftiness of the enemy, Lord,[2] and prepare me to stand against him in your faith and power. Thank you for showing me that there is indeed a warfare taking place, and that I am not wrestling against flesh and blood, but against principalities, powers, the rulers of the darkness of this world, and spiritual wickedness in high places.[3]

Through your power, I will be sober and vigilant, Father, while I wear your armor because I realize that my adversary, the devil, walks about as a roaring lion, seeking whom he may devour.[4] With your help, I will resist him and he will flee from me, according to your Word.[5]

Your protection keeps me safe, Lord. How grateful I am that I do not have to engage in spiritual warfare in my flesh, because the weapons you've given to me are not carnal; instead, they are mighty through you, Father, to the tearing down of every stronghold. It is your power that enables me to cast down imaginations, and every high thing that exalts itself against knowing you. Through your grace and power, I will bring every thought into captivity to obedience to you.[6]

Thank you for the spiritual power you are imparting to me, Father, and for the protection your armor gives to me.

References: (1) Ephesians 6:10-18; (2) Ephesians 4:14; (3) Ephesians 6:12; (4) 1 Peter 5:8; (5) James 4:7; (6) 2 Corinthians 10:4-5.

17. The Promise of God's Rest

Key Scripture: *"There remaineth therefore a rest to the people of God" (Heb. 4:9).*

Key Thought: Faith rests in God.

Prayer: Dear God, thank you for your wonderful Word which teaches me how to enter into your rest. Thank you for the spiritual rest you promise to your children if they will love you,[1] obey you, and believe your Word.[2]

Thank you for your invitation, Father. Your Son, Jesus Christ, my Lord, has beckoned me to come to Him when I am weary and heavy-laden, knowing that you will give me rest. I do so now, and I take your yoke upon me so I can learn of you. In you, Father, and in Jesus, I will find rest unto my soul. Thank you for the fact that your yoke is easy and your burden is light.[3]

Lord God, I love you and I believe your Word. Through your Word, I receive faith to appropriate your promises and to enter your rest.[4] Your Word tells me that those who are willing and obedient will eat the good of the land,[5] and enjoy your blessing.

When worries and fear threaten to disturb my rest, Lord, I will respond with prayer, and with great thanksgiving to you. I will turn my worries over to you, and as I do so, I will receive your wonderful peace which surpasses all understanding. Thank you for your peace and rest, and for your promise to keep my heart and mind through Christ Jesus.[6]

I cast all my cares, worries, and anxieties upon you, Father, and in return you give me your peace because you love me and care so much for me.[7] Trusting in your care, I find great rest.

How I rejoice in you, the God of all hope, because you are filling me with the joy and peace that come from believing. I abound in hope and rest through the power of the Holy Spirit.[8]

References: (1) John 14:15; (2) Hebrews 4:1-3; (3) Matthew 11:28-30; (4) Romans 10:17; (5) Isaiah 1:19; (6) Philippians 4:6-7; (7) 1 Peter 5:7; (8) Romans 15:13.

18. Knowing God's Will

Key Scripture: *"For this cause we also, since the day we heard it, do not cease to pray for you, and to desire that ye might be filled with the knowledge of his will in all wisdom and spiritual understanding"* *(Col. 1:9).*

Key Thought: God's Word and His will are one.

Prayer: I delight to do your will, O Lord my God, and I shall keep your Word within my heart.[1] I will guard and protect my heart with all diligence, for out of it flow the springs of life.[2]

I pray, Father, and I desire that you would fill me with the knowledge of your will in all wisdom and spiritual understanding so that I may walk worthy of you, be pleasing to you, and be fruitful in every good work.[3]

Thank you, wonderful Father, for giving me an abundance of wisdom and understanding through your Word. You have made known unto me the mystery of your will, according to your good pleasure.[4]

Father, I love you, and I love your Word. I will not let your Word depart from my mouth, but I will meditate upon it day and night. Through your grace, I will observe and do according to all that is written therein. Thank you for your promise, O Lord, that, as

I obey your will, you will make my way prosperous and give me good success.[5]

References: *(1) Psalms 40:8; (2) Proverbs 4:23; (3) Colossians 1:9-10; (4) Ephesians 1:8-9; (5) Joshua 1:8.*

19. God's Word

Key Scripture: *"For the word of God is quick, and powerful, and sharper than any two-edged sword, piercing even to the dividing asunder of soul and spirit, and of the joints and marrow, and is a discerner of the thoughts and intents of the heart" (Heb. 4:12).*

Key Thought: The Bible is a road map for your life.

Prayer: Forever, O Lord, your Word is settled in heaven.[1] I bless you because you have given me rest according to all that you have promised to me. Not one word of all your good promises has ever failed.[2] In light of this truth, I will walk in your Word at all times.

I love your Word, Father, it is a lamp unto my feet, and a light unto my path.[3] All of your words are pure, O God, and you are a shield to me.[4] Lord God, your way is perfect, and your Word is tried. You are a shield and a mighty buckler to me as I trust in you.[5]

With your Word you made the heavens, O Lord.[6] All of your promises are yes in Christ, unto your glory, O God.[7] You have spoken through your Word since ancient times,[8] in order to give light to those who sit in darkness, and you guide my feet in the way of peace.[9]

Your Word is quick, alive, and powerful, and sharper than any two-edged sword. It pierces even to the dividing asunder of my soul and spirit, and of my joints and marrow, and is a discerner of the thoughts and intents of my heart.[10]

Father, I am thankful for your Word, and I will endeavor to walk in the light of your Word all the days of my life.

References: *(1) Psalms 119:89; (2) 1 Kings 8:56; (3) Psalms 119:105; (4) Proverbs 30:5; (5) Psalms 18:30; (6) Psalms 33:6; (7) 2 Corinthians 1:20; (8) Luke 1:70; (9) Luke 1:79; (10) Hebrews 4:12.*

20. Walking in God's Word

Key Scripture: *"But he answered and said, It is written, Man shall not live by bread alone, but by every word that proceedeth out of the mouth of God" (Matt. 4:4).*

Key Thought: Walking in the Word is a joyful journey.

Prayer: Lord God, your Word is a lamp unto my feet and a light unto my path.[1] When I go, your Word will lead me. When I sleep, your Word will keep me. When I awaken, your Word will talk with me.[2] Your Word is truly a lamp and a light for me.[3]

Thank you for your Word which imparts faith to my heart.[4] As I believe your Word, you fill me with all joy and peace, and I abound in hope through the power of the Holy Spirit.[5]

Therefore, I will not let your Word depart from my mouth as I meditate upon its truths day and night. I will walk in your Word daily, and I know you will fulfill your promise to make my way prosperous, and to fill my life with good success.[6]

Dear God, your wonderful Word gives me life[7] because it is the Word of life. It reminds me that death and life are in the power of my tongue,[8] and that when I speak your Word, I speak forth life into my own heart and the hearts of others. As I continue to hold forth your Word, Lord, help me to rejoice as in the day of Christ, knowing that my labor is never in vain in you, Father.[9] Help me to always be a doer of your Word, not only a hearer.[10] By keeping your Word, I realize that your love is made perfect in me. give me your grace, Lord, to be both a doer and a keeper of your Word.[11]

Lord God, your way is perfect, and your Word is tried. You are my mighty buckler, and I put all my trust in you.[12] I know your Word will never return to you without it having its desired effect.[13] Thank you for your Word, Father, and help me to keep on walking in your Word.

Heavenly Father, I want to live by every word that comes from your mouth.[14] Your Word is wonderful to me; it is quick, powerful, and sharper than any two-edged sword.[15] I will walk in the light of your Word every day of my life.

References: (1) Psalms 119:105; (2) Proverbs 6:22-23; (3) Proverbs 6:23; (4) Romans 10:17; (5) Romans 15:13; (6) Joshua 1:8; (7) Psalms 119:150; (8) Proverbs 18:21; (9) Philippians 2:16; (10) James 1:22; (11) 1 John 2:5; (12) Psalms 18:30; (13) Isaiah 55:10-12; (14) Matthew 4:4; (15) Hebrews 4:12.*

21. Walking in Goodness

Key Scripture: *"For ye were sometimes darkness, but now are ye light in the Lord: walk as children of light: For the fruit of the Spirit is in all goodness and righteousness and truth" (Eph. 5:8-9).*

Key Thought: Goodness is a fruit of the Spirit.

Prayer: Thank you, O God, for the precious faith I have obtained through your righteousness. You are multiplying your grace and peace unto me through my knowledge of you and Jesus, my Lord, for your divine power has given me all things that pertain to life and godliness.[1]

You have given me the great and precious promises of your Word so that by them I might be a partaker of your divine nature, and thereby escape the corruption that is in the world.[2] This makes me so very thankful, Father.

As a partaker of your divine nature, through the indwelling of your Holy Spirit,[3] I am able to walk in the fruit of goodness.[4] Therefore, giving all diligence, I will add virtue to my faith, and knowledge to my virtue. To my knowledge, I will add self-control, and to my self-control, I will add patience. To my patience, I will add godliness, and to my godliness, I will add kindness. To my kindness, I will add love.[5] As I let these qualities develop in my life, I will be able to walk in goodness at all times.

Thank you, O Lord, for your promise that these qualities will make me fruitful in the knowledge of Jesus Christ, my Savior and Lord.[6]

References: *(1) 2 Peter 1:1-3; (2) 2 Peter 1:4; (3) John 14:17; (4) Galatians 5:22; (5) 2 Peter 1:5-7; (6) 2 Peter 1:8.*

22. Spiritual Growth

Key Scripture: *"As newborn babes, desire the sincere milk of the word, that ye may grow thereby" (1 Pet. 2:2).*

Key Thought: God's Word is food for growth.

Prayer: Thank you, Father, for showing me that as I desire and drink the sincere milk of your Word I will grow spiritually.[1]   All Scripture has been given by your inspiration,[2] and I want to live by every word that proceeds from your mouth.[3]   I will study your Word so that I will never need to be ashamed, because I will know how to rightly divide your Word of truth.[4]

As I walk in the light of your Word,[5] Father, I will meditate upon your precepts, and give myself totally to them.[6] Speaking the truth in love, I will grow up into Christ in all things.[7] Father, I deeply desire to fully know the love of Christ, which surpasses knowledge, so that I would be filled with all your fullness.[8]

I rejoice, O Lord, in the promise of your Word that tells me that I will flourish like the palm tree, and grow like a cedar in Lebanon.[9] My delight, dear Father, is in your Word, and in your Word I will meditate day and night. You assure me that this will cause me to be like a tree planted by the rivers of water, that brings forth its fruit in its season, and whatever I do shall prosper.[10]

Thank you, Father, for helping me to grow in grace, and in the knowledge of my Lord and Savior, Jesus Christ. To Him be glory forevermore.[11]

References: (1) 1 Peter 2:2; (2) 2 Timothy 3:16; (3) Matthew 4:4; (4) 2 Timothy 2:15; (5) Psalms 119:105; (6) 1 Timothy 4:15; (7) Ephesians 4:15; (8) Ephesians 3:19; (9) Psalms 92:12-13; (10) Psalms 1:2-3; (11) 2 Peter 3:18.

23. Walking in Holiness

Key Scripture: *"Having therefore these promises, dearly beloved, let us cleanse ourselves from all filthiness of the flesh and spirit, perfecting holiness in the fear of God"* (2 Cor. 7:1).

Key Thought: God's will for us is holiness.

Prayer: Holy, holy, holy, are you, Lord God almighty.[1] O God, I exalt you, and I worship you, for you are holy.[2] I glory in your holy name, and my heart rejoices.[3] Glory and honor are in your presence, O God, and strength and gladness are in your sanctuary. I ascribe glory and strength to you. I will forever give unto you the glory that is due your name, and I worship you in the beauty of holiness.[4]

Thank you, Father-God, for blessing me with every spiritual blessing in heavenly places in Christ. I thank you, also, that you chose me in Him before the foundation of the world so that I would be holy and blameless before you in love.[5]

Father, thank you for your divine power which has given me all things that pertain to life and godliness through knowing you and the Lord Jesus Christ. Thank you for calling me to glory and virtue, and for giving me your exceedingly great and precious promises which enable me to be a partaker of your divine nature.[6] This astounding truth is what enables me to walk in holiness. Thank you, Father.

References: *(1) Revelation 4:8; (2) Psalms 99:9; (3) Psalms 105:3; (4) 1 Chronicles 16:27-29; (5) Ephesians 1:3-4; (6) 2 Peter 1:3-4.*

24. Being Filled With the Holy Spirit

Key Scripture: *"Be filled with the Spirit" (Eph. 5:18).*

Key Thought: The Holy Spirit fills to overflowing.

Prayer: Heavenly Father, I desire to be filled with your Holy Spirit. Thank you for sending the Holy Spirit who is the divine Comforter, the Spirit of truth.[1] Thank you for your promise to give the Holy spirit to all who ask you.[2] Fill me to overflowing with your Spirit, Lord, as I wait before you now.[3]

As I open my heart by faith, Lord, I believe that I receive your Holy Spirit now,[4] and I want to live in such a way that I would never grieve Him.[5] What a blessing it is to realize that the same Spirit that raised my Lord Jesus Christ from the dead dwells in me.[6] I thank you that the Holy Spirit will abide with me forever.[7]

Because your Spirit dwells within me, Lord, I am able to be led by Him.[8] Your Holy Spirit bears witness with my spirit that I am your child.[9] Thank you for filling me with your Spirit, Father.

References: (1) John 14:16; (2) Luke 11:13; (3) Acts 13:52; (4) Mark 11:24; (5) John 20:22; (6) Romans 8:11; (7) John 14:16; (8) Romans 8:14; (9) Romans 8:16.

25. **Humility**

Key Scripture: *"Be clothed with humility: for God resisteth the proud, and giveth grace to the humble. Humble yourselves therefore under the mighty hand of God, that he may exalt you in due time" (1 Pet. 5:5-6).*

Key Thought: Humility is one of the finest garments.

Prayer: Father, thank you for Jesus' example of humility. I want to take His yoke upon me and to learn from Him, for He is meek and lowly of heart.[1] It amazes me to realize that though He is one with you, He made himself of no reputation, and took upon himself the form of a servant, and was made in the likeness of men. And being found in fashion as a man, He humbled himself, and became obedient unto death on the cross. Because of His humble obedience, you have highly exalted Him, and I rejoice in His name which is above every name.[2]

It is humbling to me to realize that you have adopted me as your child,[3] and, like Jesus, I want never to let anything I do be done through strife or selfish motives, but in lowliness of mind, I will serve others.[4] Grant me the humble heart of a servant, Lord, so I may be more like Jesus.

It is you, Father, who is at work within me both to will and to do your good pleasure.[5] I thank you that I am your workmanship, created in Christ Jesus unto the good works you desire.[6]

Father, I humble myself under your almighty hand,[7] and I ask you now to clothe me with the humility[8] of Christ so that His mind will be in me[9] and guide me in all that I do.

References: (1) Matthew 11:29; (2) Philippians 2:5-9; (3) Ephesians 1:5; (4) Philippians 2:3; (5) Philippians 2:13; (6) Ephesians 2:10; (7) 1 Peter 5:6; (8) 1 Peter 5:5; (9) Philippians 2:5.

26. Walking in Integrity

Key Scripture: *"The integrity of the upright shall guide them: but the perverseness of transgressors shall destroy them" (Prov. 11:3).*

Key Thought: Christian character includes personal integrity.

Prayer: Dear God, I desire to walk in integrity, and to follow its guidance in my life by always choosing to do what is right.[1] As you help me to be true to what I know is right, I will be able to walk in the integrity of my heart.[2]

Therefore, as I endeavor to walk in integrity, I will let the word of Christ dwell in me richly, in all wisdom, and whatever I do in word or in deed, I will do all in the name of the Lord Jesus, giving thanks to you, Father, by Him.[3] I realize that this is a key to personal integrity in my life.

O God, keep my soul, and deliver me. Let me not be ashamed, for I put my trust in you. Let integrity and uprightness preserve me, for I wait on you.[4]

Show me your ways, O Lord, and teach me your paths. Lead me in your truth, and teach me, for you are the God of my salvation, and I wait on you.[5]

Your Word is truth,[6] dear Father, and it guides me. Your Word is a lamp unto my feet, and a light unto my path,[7] and I will walk in the light of your Word.

Thank you for upholding me in my integrity.[8]

References: *(1) Proverbs 11:3; (2) Genesis 20:6; (3) Colossians 3:16-17; (4) Psalms 25:20-21; (5) Psalms 25:4-5; (6) John 17:17; (7) Psalms 119:105; (8) Psalms 41:12.*

27. Who Jesus Is to You

Key Scripture: *"Jesus saith unto him, I am the way, the truth, and the life: no man cometh unto the Father, but by me" (John 14:6).*

Key Thought: All your needs are met in Jesus Christ.

Prayer: Lord Jesus, you are my Shepherd, and because this is true, I know I shall never want for anything. You make me to lie down in green pastures, and you lead me beside the still waters. You restore my soul, and you lead me in the paths of righteousness for your name's sake.[1]

Though I walk through the valley of the shadow of death, I will fear no evil, for you are with me. Your rod and your staff are a comfort to me. You prepare a table before me in the presence of my enemies. You anoint my head with oil, and my cup overflows.[2]

Surely goodness and mercy will follow me all the days of my life, and I will dwell in your house forever.[3]

Jesus, I love you. You are my Lord,[4] and my Savior.[5] You gave your life for me,[6] and your blood cleanses me from all my sins.[7] Your truth sets me free.[8]

You were wounded for my transgressions. You were bruised for my iniquities, and with your stripes I am healed and made whole.[9]

I worship you Lord Jesus. I believe that you are the Son of God[10] who was raised from the dead so that I might be justified.[11] In you all things hold together,[12] and through your strength I can do all things.[13] You give me authority over all the power of the enemy.[14] You are the Alpha and the Omega, the beginning and the end, the first and the last, forever.[15]

Lord Jesus, you are truly everything to me.

References: *(1) Psalms 23:1-3; (2) Psalms 23:4-5; (3) Psalms 23:6; (4) Romans 5:1; (5) Luke 2:11; (6) Galatians 2:20; (7) John 1:7; (8) John 8:32; (9) Isaiah 53:5; (10) Romans 1:4; (11) Romans 4:25; (12) Colossians 1:17; (13) Philippians 4:13; (14) Luke 10:19; (15) Revelation 1:8.*

28. The Joy of the Lord

Key Scripture: *"Do not sorrow, for the joy of the Lord is your strength"* (Neh. 8:10, NKJV).

Key Thought: Circumstances are not your master.

Prayer: Your joy, O Lord, bubbles up within my soul from the inner wellspring that comes from knowing you.[1] Your joy floods my spirit, soul, and body. It fills my mind with happiness.[2] I sing with joy[3] when I realize who you are, Father, and when I contemplate all you have done for me and mine, my excitement intensifies.[4]

Thank you for the joy you've imparted to me.[5] You are my highest joy, and you are my delight.[6] I will walk in the strength your joy imparts to me,[7] and as I ask and receive in Jesus' name, I know my joy will be full.[8] Thank you, Lord.

My joy is complete when I pray in the authority represented by Jesus' name, because I know that you, Father, will hear and answer all my prayers.[9] Your abiding joy is my ever-lasting strength.[10] Your joy goes so much deeper than anything this world has to offer.[11] It is far more wonderful than any human emotion. Like a fountain that springs from the depths of the earth, your joy rises and fills me; then it flows forth from my life and touches all those with whom I come in contact.[12]

I receive your wonderful joy as I pray, dear Father.

References: *(1) Isaiah 12:3; (2) Isaiah 61:7; (3) Psalms 67:4; (4) 1 Thessalonians 5:16; (5) 1 Thessalonians 5:18; (6) Psalms 43:4; (7) Nehemiah 8:10; (8) John 16:24; (9) John 16:23; (10) Nehemiah 8:10; (11) Psalms 43:4; (12) Isaiah 55:12.*

29. Knowing God Better

Key Scripture: *"That ye might walk worthy of the Lord unto all pleasing, being fruitful in every good work, and increasing in the knowledge of God" (Col. 1:10).*

Key Thought: God wants to be your closest friend.

Prayer: Lord God, I serve you with gladness, and I come before your presence with singing. I know that you are my God. It is you who made me; and not myself. I am your child, and I am a sheep in your pasture. I enter your gates with thanksgiving, and I go into your courts with praise. I am so thankful to you, and I bless your name, because you are good, and your mercy is everlasting. Father, I thank you that your truth endures to all generations.[1]

I want to know you better, Father, and therefore I will call upon you, knowing that you will hearken unto me; and I will seek you, knowing I will find you, for I will seek you with all my heart.[2] As I pursue knowing you better, O God, I will draw near to you, and I know you will draw near to me.[3]

Father, I desire to experience a deeper and more intimate fellowship with you, and I thank you that you desire that as well. I rejoice that you have made it possible for me to have close fellowship with you, Father, and with your Son, Jesus Christ.[4]

Dear Father, I am excited as I look forward in eager anticipation of getting to know you better and better.

References: *(1) Psalms 100-2-5; (2) Jeremiah 29:12-13; (3) James 4:8; (4) 1 John 1:3.*

30. Walking in Love

Key Scripture: *"Be ye therefore followers of God, as dear children; And walk in love, as Christ also hath loved us, and hath given himself for us an offering and a sacrifice to God for a sweetsmelling savour" (Eph. 5:1-2).*

Key Thought: Love never fails. (See 1 Cor. 13:8.)

Prayer: Loving God and Father, thank you for your limitless love which is from everlasting to everlasting.[1] Thank you for pouring your love abroad in my heart through your Holy Spirit which has been given to me.[2] Because you have shown me that you are love,[3] and that love is the most excellent way,[4] I choose to obey you by walking in love as Christ has loved me.[5]

Thank you, Father, for giving me love as a fruit of the Holy Spirit [6] who dwells within me.[7] Through His power, I will walk in love. Grant me the grace to be patient and kind, to love others without envy or jealousy, to not be puffed up and haughty, to not behave rudely, and to not ever be self-seeking.[8]

Through the power of your grace and love, I will walk in love, rejoicing in the truth, bearing up under all circumstances, always believing and trusting, always hoping, and always enduring all things.[9]

Father-God, I thank you that love never fails.[10]   I will always eagerly pursue this love.[11] Beginning today, Father, I will make walking in love my great quest.

References: *(1) Jeremiah 31:3; (2) Romans 5:5; (3) 1 John 4:8; (4) 1 Corinthians 12:31; (5) Ephesians 5:2; (6) Galatians 5:22; (7) John 14:17; (8) 1 Corinthians 13:4-5; (9) 1 Corinthians 13:6-7; (10) 1 Corinthians 13:8; (11) 1 Corinthians 14:1.*

31. Walking in Meekness

Key Scripture: *"Take my yoke upon you, and learn of me; for I am meek and lowly in heart: and ye shall find rest unto your souls"* (Matt. 11:29).

Key Thought: Never confuse meekness with weakness.

Prayer: Heavenly Father, I want to walk in the fruit of meekness.[1] You promise amazing things to the meek, for you tell me that the meek will inherit the earth and experience deep and abiding joy.[2] Let this fruit of your Spirit grow in me daily as I choose to walk worthy of your calling in my life with meekness of heart.[3] Through your grace, Father, I choose to walk in an attitude of complete humility, meekness, and patience, always bearing with others through love.[4]

Father, I want to be like Jesus who is meek and lowly in heart. I willingly take His yoke upon me, and I will learn from Him, and this will give me rest.[5] Thank you, God. Father, with joy in my heart, I now put on the new person, which is being renewed in knowledge after your image.[6]

I praise you, O God, that I am your workmanship in Christ Jesus for good works, which you have prepared for me to walk in.[7] I surrender to your working, O God, as you cultivate the fruit of meekness in my life.

References: *(1) Galatians 5:23; (2) Matthew 5:5; (3) Ephesians 4:1; (4) Ephesians 4:2; (5) Matthew 11:29; (6) Colossians 3:10; (7) Ephesians 2:10.*

32. The New Birth

Key Scripture: *"Being born again, not of corruptible seed, but of incorruptible, by the word of God, which liveth and abideth for ever"* (1 Pet. 1:23).

Key Thought: You are a new creation.

Prayer: Heavenly Father, thank you for providing me with eternal life through your Son, my Lord and Savior, Jesus Christ. In the same way that Jesus rose from the dead, you have allowed me to rise up and walk in newness of life with you[1] as I trust Christ for salvation. Thank you for the joy of salvation that my faith gives to me.[2] Help me always to serve you in newness of spirit.[3]

Father, you have enabled me, through faith, to be in Christ, and this has made me an entirely new creation in Him.[4] Thank you for letting the old things pass away and for letting all things become new in my life.[5] With a thankful heart, I put on the new man, which is created in righteousness and true holiness after you, Lord.[6]

By your boundless mercy, I have been begotten (been born again) to a living hope through the Resurrection of Jesus Christ from the dead.[7] Yes, Lord, I have been born again of incorruptible seed by your Word.[8]

Because I have believed in Christ as my Savior you have enabled me to be born into your family.[9] Thank you, Father. Because I have been born of you, I am now able to overcome the world through faith.[10] Through your grace, I firmly place your helmet of salvation upon my head as I take up the shield of faith which is able to quench all the fiery darts of the enemy.[11]

Thank you, Father, for saving me and keeping me.

References: (1) Romans 6:4; (2) Psalms 51:12; (3) Romans 7:6; (4) Galatians 6:15; (5) 2 Corinthians 5:17; (6) Ephesians 4:24; (7) 1 Peter 1:3-5; (8) 1 Peter 1:23; (9) 1 John 4:15; (10) 1 John 5:4; (11) Ephesians 6:16-17.

33. Obedience

Key Scripture: *"If you are willing and obedient, you shall eat the good of the land" (Isa. 1:19, NKJV).*

Key Thought: Obedience is a life style.

Prayer: Dear God, I love you and I want to obey you. I'm thrilled with your Word that teaches me that as I obey you and keep your words, I will experience your love, and you will make your abode with me.[1] Your abiding presence gives me fullness of joy,[2] and inspires me to obey you more and more.

As I ponder the importance of obedience in my life, Lord, I am truly stunned by your promise which tells me that if I will obey your voice and keep your covenant, I will become your special treasure.[3] Your Word teaches me that all your promises are yes to me, in Christ Jesus.[4]

Please forgive me, Lord, for each time when I have disobeyed you in any way. I truly repent of all disobedience in my life.

Show me your ways, O Lord, and teach me your paths. Lead me in your truth, and teach me, for you are the God of my salvation.[5] Let your Spirit guide me into all truth, according to your Word.[6]

I now surrender to your will in all things,[7] as I commit myself to obeying you.

References: *(1) John 14:23; (2) Psalms 16:11; (3) Exodus 19:5; (4) 2 Corinthians 1:20; (5) Psalms 25:4-5; (6) John 16:13; (7) Luke 22:42.*

34. Praying More Effectively

Key Scripture: *"And this is the confidence that we have in him, that, if we ask any thing according to his will, he heareth us" (1 John 5:14).*

Key Thought: God is never more than a prayer away.

Prayer: Lord God, thank you for the promise of your Word that tells me when I call unto you, you will answer me, and show me great and mighty things.[1] This wonderful promise inspires me to learn to pray more effectively and to experience all you have for me in prayer.

I thank you, Father, for the confidence I have in you, that, if I ask anything according to your will, you do hear me. And because I know you hear me, I know that I will receive whatever petitions I ask of you.[2] Your Word reveals your will to me;[3] therefore, I will pray according to your Word.

Your Word is filled with so many precious prayer promises. Thank you, Lord, for each one. As I meditate on these promises, and learn to pray your Word and your will, I know your Word will never return unto you void. It will always accomplish your purposes.[4] Thank you, Father.

Thank you for your Holy Spirit who helps me to pray more effectively, for when I'm not sure how to pray about a matter, the

Spirit comes to my aid.[5] I trust the Holy
Spirit to lead and help me in every area of my
life, including prayer.[6]

Father, I thank you for teaching me how
to pray more effectively.

References: *(1) Jeremiah 33:3; (2) 1 John 5:14-15;
(3) 2 Timothy 3:16; (4) Isaiah 55:11; (5) Romans
8:26; (6) Romans 8:14.*

35. Living in the Present

Key Scripture: *"Take therefore no thought for the morrow: for the morrow shall take thought for the things of itself. Sufficient unto the day is the evil thereof"* (Matt. 6:34).

Key Thought: Each new day is a gift of God.

Prayer: Heavenly Father, thank you for today, a day which you have made. I will rejoice and be glad in it.[1] Forgetting those things that are behind, and reaching forth unto those things which are before, I press toward the mark for the prize of the high calling of God in Christ Jesus.[2] You are my ever-present help, O Lord.[3]

Because you are always there, I will set you continually before me. Because you are at my right hand, I will not be moved. Therefore, my heart is glad, and my glory rejoices in you, Father, and I will rest in your hope.[4] You are showing me the path of life each step of the way, O Lord. In your presence I find fullness of joy every moment of this day, and at your right hand I experience pleasures forevermore.[5] Thank you, Father.

Give me your grace to make the most of every moment today, and help me to seize every opportunity that comes my way. I will redeem the time today, and I will walk purposefully and wisely as you reveal your will to me.[6]

Today, dear Father, I will trust in you with all my heart, leaning not to my own understanding.   In all my ways, I will acknowledge you, and I know you will direct my paths.[7]

References: *(1) Psalms 118:24; (2) Philippians 3:13-14; (3) Psalms 46:1; (4) Psalms 16:8-9; (5) Psalms 16:11; (6) Ephesians 5:16-17; (7) Proverbs 3:5-6.*

36. A Prayer of Rejoicing

Key Scripture: *"Rejoice in the Lord, O ye righteous: for praise is comely for the upright" (Ps. 33:1).*

Key Thought: Rejoicing is our response to God's goodness.

Prayer: Dear Father, I trust in you and I rejoice. I will shout for joy forever, because you defend me. I love your name, and I am joyful in you, for I know you, Lord, will bless me, and with your favor you will surround me like a shield.[1]

Thank you, Lord God, that your eye is upon me. You have delivered me from death. I wait upon you because you are my help and my shield. My heart rejoices in you, because I have trusted in your holy name.[2] Because you have been my help, in the shadow of your wings I will rejoice.[3] O Lord, I will rejoice in you with praise. I will bless you at all times. Your praise will be continually in my mouth.[4] Blessed be your name from this time forth and forevermore. From the rising of the sun unto the going down of the same, your name will be praised.[5]

My heart is fixed, O God, my heart is fixed. I will sing and give praise. I will wake up early and praise you, O Lord, among the people.[6]

I will rejoice in you always, Lord,[7] and
with joy I will draw water from your wells of
salvation.[8]

References: *(1) Psalms 5:11-12; (2) Psalms 33:18-21;*
(3) Psalms 63:7; (4) Psalms 34:1; (5) Psalms 113:2-3;
(6) Psalms 57:7-9; (7) Philippians 4:4; (8) Isaiah 12:3.

37. When You Need to Rejoice

Key Scripture: *"That the trial of your faith, being much more precious than of gold that perisheth, though it be tried with fire, might be found unto praise and honour and glory at the appearing of Jesus Christ: Whom having not seen, ye love; in whom, though now ye see him not, yet believing, ye rejoice with joy unspeakable and full of glory"* (1 Pet. 1:7-8).

Key Thought: Rejoicing is enjoying God and His goodness to us.

Prayer: Heavenly Father, I rejoice in you with exceedingly great joy because of all you've done for me and because of who you are.[1] Indeed, in everything I give you thanks, because I know this is your will for me. Help me, Lord, to rejoice evermore, and to pray without ceasing.[2]

Alleluia! I rejoice in you, Father, because you reign forever. This gives me great gladness of heart; therefore, I rejoice, and give honor unto you![3] You alone are worthy to receive honor and glory, O Lord.[4] I choose to magnify and exalt you as I enter your gates with thanksgiving and proceed into your courts with praise.[5]

Thank you for being my Lord and my God. Thank you for working your purposes out in my life and through my life. I make a joyful noise unto you as I serve you with growing gladness. I come before your presence with singing. I am thankful for knowing that you are my Lord. It is you who made me, and I am your child. Praise your mighty name![6]

Thank you for everything, Father. I bless your name because you are good. Your mercy is everlasting, and your truth endures to all generations.[7] Thank you.

You are so great, dear God, and you are greatly to be praised.[8] I will bless you with all that I have within me.[9]

I bless your most holy name as I rejoice in you.[10]

References: *(1) Philippians 3:1; (2) 1 Thessalonians 5:16-18; (3) Revelation 19:6-7; (4) Revelation 4:11; (5) Psalms 100:4; (6) Psalms 100:3; (7) Psalms 117:2; (8) Psalms 48:1; (9) Psalms 103:1; (10) Psalms 34:1-3.*

38. The Need to Renew Your Mind

Key Scripture: *"And do not be conformed to this world, but be transformed by the renewing of your mind, that you may prove what is that good and acceptable and perfect will of God" (Rom. 12:2, NKJV).*

Key Thought: God will renew your mind through His Word.

Prayer: Father-God, your Word shows me that to be spiritually minded gives me life and peace.[1] I want to have my mind renewed, and I thank you that you will keep me in perfect peace as I keep my mind focused on you.[2]

I choose not to be conformed to this world, but to be transformed by the renewal of my mind so that I will be able to walk in your good, acceptable, and perfect will.[3]

I will let the mind of Christ be in me.[4] I thank you, Father, that I am crucified with Christ; nevertheless I live; yet it is not I, but Christ, who lives in me, and the life I now live in the flesh, I live by faith in the Son of God who loved me, and gave himself for me.[5]

As I pray, I realize I am being renewed in the spirit of my mind,[6] and I am being sanctified and cleansed by washing in the water of your Word.[7]

The entrance of your words, O God, gives me light.[8] Your Word is true.[9] As I receive the truth of your Word, it sets me free from a worldly mind-set.[10]

Thank you, Father, for renewing my mind.

References: *(1) Romans 8:6; (2) Isaiah 26:3; (3) Romans 12:2; (4) Philippians 2:5; (5) Galatians 2:20; (6) Ephesians 4:23; (7) Ephesians 5:26; (8) Psalms 119:130; (9) John 17:17; (10) John 8:32.*

39. Walking in Revelation

Key Scripture: *"Now we have received, not the spirit of the world, but the Spirit who is from God, that we might know the things that have been freely given to us by God" (1 Cor. 2:12, NKJV).*

Key Thought: God loves to reveal His truth to His children.

Prayer: Lord God, you are the God who knows all things, and I desire to walk in your revelation. Thank you for your promise that when I call unto you, you will answer me and show me great and mighty thing.[1] I ask you to give me the spirit of wisdom and revelation in the knowledge of you. Enlighten the eyes of my understanding so that I will know the hope of your calling, and what are the riches of your glorious inheritance in the saints.

Thank you for your promise that you will reveal to me the exceeding greatness of your power toward me as a believer, according to the working of your mighty power, which you wrought in Christ when you raised Him from the dead, and set him at your own right hand in the heavenly places, far above all principality, might, power, dominion, and every name that is named, not only in this world, but also in that which is to come.

Thank you, Father, for putting all things under His feet, and for giving Him the power to be the Head over all things to the Church, which is His body, the fullness of Him which fills all in all. Amen.[2]

References: *(1) Jeremiah 33:3; (2) Ephesians 1:17-23.*

40. Revival

Key Scripture: *"For the earth shall be filled with the knowledge of the glory of the Lord, as the waters cover the sea" (Hab. 2:14).*

Key Thought: Earnest prayer paves the way for revival.

Prayer: Lord God, thank you for all the promises of your Word which give me hope for revival. Your Word is alive and dynamic, and it is sharper than any two-edged sword, piercing even to the division of soul and spirit, and of joints and marrow, and it is a discerner of the thoughts and intents of the human heart.[1] Let your Word have its work in my life, Father. Create in me a pure heart, O God, and renew a steadfast spirit within me.[2]

I ask you to hasten the day when the earth will be filled with the knowledge of your glory, as the waters cover the sea.[3] I know, dear Father, that it is not your will for anyone to perish. You want all people, everywhere, to come to repentance, and I believe your promises of revival.[4] Therefore, I will patiently watch and wait for your coming as a farmer waits for the fruit of the earth to come forth, after the early and latter rains.[5] Bring forth the latter rain of your Spirit upon earth, O God.

It excites me to anticipate the day when you will pour out your Spirit upon all flesh. Thank you for that stirring promise, Father. I believe that revival is imminent, and when it happens, the young men and women will prophesy, old men will dream dreams, and young men will see visions.[6] You, Lord God, will make bare your holy arm for all the world to see, and all the ends of the earth will see your salvation.[7] I seek your promised revival, Lord.

When the revival fires you promise are ignited, Father, you will do a new thing in our midst. You will make a way in the wilderness, and rivers in the desert.[8] Thank you, Lord God. You will seek that which was lost, and bring again that which was driven away. You will bind up that which was broken, and you will strengthen that which was sick. You will decree your judgment upon the people of the earth.[9]

Lord, I ask you to usher in the end-time revival you have promised to your people. I look forward to that glorious revival with zeal and faith. I believe it will cause all the ends of the world to remember you and to turn toward you. All the nations will worship before you, because your's is the Kingdom, Father.[10] My Father in heaven, your name is hallowed. I pray that your kingdom will come, and your will shall be done, on earth as it is in heaven, for yours is the Kingdom, the power, and the glory forever. Amen.[11]

References: (1) *Hebrews 4:12;* (2) *Psalms 51:10;*
(3) *Habakkuk 2:14;* (4) *2 Peter 3:9;* (5) *James 5:7;*
(6) *Joel 2:28;* (7) *Isaiah 52:10;* (8) *Isaiah 43:19;*
(9) *Ezekiel 34:16;* (10) *Psalms 22:27-28;*
(11) *Matthew 6:9-13.*

41. Seeking God

Key Scripture: *"And ye shall seek me, and find me, when ye shall search for me with all your heart" (Jer. 29:13).*

Key Thought: Seek, and you shall find. (See Matt. 7:7.)

Prayer: Lord God, I seek you with all my heart. I want always to seek you, because I know that I will surely find you when I seek your face continually.[1] As I draw near to you now, I know you are drawing near to me.[2] You are my God, and I will seek you early,[3] Father, for my soul thirsts for you, and I desire to see your power and your glory revealed. Your lovingkindness is better than life to me. Therefore, my lips will praise you, and I will bless you at all times.[4] My heart rejoices as I seek you. I will glory in your holy name as I seek you and your strength.[5]

Thank you for your promise that when I call upon you, you will answer me and show me great and mighty things which I do not know.[6] When I ask, I will receive. When I seek, I will find. When I knock it shall be opened unto me.[7]

O God, I give thanks unto you as I call upon your name. I will declare your deeds among the people. I will sing praises unto you, and talk of all your wondrous works. I glory in your holy name, and my heart rejoices as I seek you. Therefore, I will seek you and your strength continually as I remember your marvelous works, wonders, and words.[8]

Thank you, Lord God, for the joy and strength I receive from seeking you. You are truly a Rewarder of those who diligently seek you.[9]

References: (1) Deuteronomy 4:29; (2) James 4:8; (3) Psalms 63:1; (4) Psalms 63:1-3; (5) Psalms 105:3-4; (6) Jeremiah 33:3; (7) Matthew 7:7; (8) 1 Chronicles 16:8-12; (9) Hebrews 11:6.

42. Walking in Self-Control

Key Scripture: *"He that hath no rule over his own spirit is like a city that is broken down, and without walls" (Prov. 25:28).*

Key Thought: Self-control (temperance) is a fruit of the Spirit. (See Gal. 5:23.)

Prayer: Dear God, thank you for your power which has given me all things that pertain to life and godliness.[1] You teach me that godliness is profitable and valuable in every way, for it holds promise for my present life and the life which is to come.[2] I want to obey you, Father, by being a godly person who exercises self-control at all times.

I confess that too many times I've failed to practice self-control, and I recognize my need to have the fruit of self-control manifested in my life through the power of your Holy Spirit.[3] Father, I repent for the many times when I have acted inappropriately by failing to exercise self-control, and I thank you for forgiving me and cleansing me of all unrighteousness.[4]

I take delight, dear God, in your exceedingly great and precious promises whereby you have made me a partaker of your divine nature, through which you enable me to escape the corruption of the world.[5]

In all diligence, Father, I will exercise faith in your promises so that I may grow in virtue, knowledge, and self-control. In this way, I know you will help me to develop greater patience, kindness, and to exercise godliness in all areas of my life.[6]

Dear Lord, I thank you for the fruit of self-control which is growing in my life.

References: *(1) 2 Peter 1:3; (2) 1 Timothy 4:8; (3) Galatians 5:23; (4) 1 John 1:9; (5) 2 Peter 1:4; (6) 2 Peter 1:5-7.*

43. Authority Over the Enemy

Key Scripture: *"And they overcame him by the blood of the Lamb, and by the word of their testimony, and they loved not their lives unto the death" (Rev. 12:11).*

Key Thought: Resist the devil, and he will flee from you. (See James 4:7.)

Prayer: Heavenly Father, thank you for the authority you have given to me to be victorious over the enemy in every area of my life. Through the authority given to me through the blood of Jesus[1], your most holy Word[2], your Holy Spirit[3], unfeigned faith[4], and the blessed name of Jesus Christ[5], I will always prevail over the enemy. Hallelujah! I am more than a conqueror through Jesus Christ who loved me.[6]

With your continuing help, Lord God, I will be sober and vigilant, because I realize that Satan, as a roaring lion, is walking about, seeking whom he may devour. I will resist him, steadfast in the faith.[7] I submit myself to you, Father, and I resist the devil. Therefore, I know he is fleeing from me.[8] Thank you, God.

Above all, I take the shield of faith — your mighty Word — and I use it to quench all the fiery darts that the enemy hurls in my direction.[9] I will overcome him at all times through the blood of the Lamb and the word of my testimony.[10] I will refuse to believe every spirit, and I will try the spirits to see whether they are from you.[11]

How I praise you, Father, for the realization that the weapons you've given to me for spiritual warfare are not carnal. Instead, they are mighty through you to the tearing down of evil strongholds. I will use the weapons you've given to cast down imaginations, and every high thing that exalts itself against knowing you, and I will bring into captivity every thought to the obedience of Christ.[12]

Thank you so much, God of peace, for bruising Satan under my feet, and for giving me the grace of my Lord Jesus Christ in all things. Amen.[13]

References: *(1) 1 John 1:7; (2) John 8:31-32; (3) Luke 24:49; (4) 2 Timothy 1:5; (5) Mark 16:17; (6) Romans 8:37; (7) 1 Peter 5:8-9; (8) James 4:7; (9) Ephesians 6:16; (10) Revelation 12:11; (11) 1 John 4:1; (12) 2 Corinthians 10:3-5; (13) Romans 16:20.*

44. Spiritual Strength

Key Scripture: *"Finally, my brethren, be strong in the Lord, and in the power of his might"* (Eph. 6:10).

Key Thought: God is my strength. (See Ps. 27:1.)

Prayer: Lord God, you are my refuge and strength, a very present help in trouble.[1] Strengthen me according to your Word.[2]

Lord, you are my light and my salvation. Whom shall I fear? You are the strength of my life; of whom shall I be afraid?[3] I thank you, Father, that nothing is too hard for you.[4]

Thank you for the multitude of promises in your Word which assure me that you will always strengthen me. Thank you for the truth that I can do all things through Christ who strengthens me.[5]

You always give power to the faint, and to them that seemingly have no might, you always increase their strength.[6]

I will wait upon you, Lord God, and as I do so, you renew my strength.[7] Being strengthened with all might, by your glorious power, I enter into the realm of patience, endurance, and joy.[8]

I pray, Father, that you would strengthen me with might by your Spirit in my innermost being[9] so that I will always be strong in you, and in the power of your might.[10]

References: *(1) Psalms 46:1; (2) Psalms 119:28; (3) Psalms 27:1; (4) Genesis 18:14; (5) Philippians 4:13; (6) Isaiah 40:29; (7) Isaiah 40:31; (8) Colossians 1:11-12; (9) Ephesians 3:16; (10) Ephesians 6:10.*

45. Trusting God

Key Scripture: *"Trust in the Lord with all thine heart; and lean not unto thine own understanding. In all thy ways acknowledge him, and he shall direct thy paths" (Prov. 3:5-6).*

Key Thought: A trusting heart enjoys God's rest. (See Heb. 4.)

Prayer: O Lord my God, in you do I put my trust.[1] Trusting you fills me with indescribable happiness and a deep, abiding joy.[2] It is my heart's desire to trust in you always and to do good. I will delight myself in you, O God, and I know you will give me the desires of my heart.[3]

As I commit my life to you, Lord, and trust in you, you will fulfill your promises to me. You will bring forth my righteousness as the light, and your judgment as the noonday. Knowing these truths enables me to rest in you.[4]

Trusting fully in you, Father, I will hold fast the profession of my faith without wavering, for I know that you are always faithful in fulfilling all your promises to me.[5]

Your Word gives me faith to trust you more, O Lord.[6] I gladly receive your words, therefore, and I hide your commands in my heart.[7] In complete confidence in you, I attend to your words, and incline my ear to your sayings. I will not let them depart from my eyes; I will keep them in the midst of my heart, for they are life and health to me.[8]

Because my heart is fixed, O God, trusting in you, I will not be afraid.[9]

References: (1) Psalms 7:1; (2) Psalms 34:8; (3) Psalms 37:3-4; (4) Psalms 37:5-7; (5) Hebrews 10:23; (6) Romans 10:17 (7) Proverbs 2:1; (8) Proverbs 4:20-22; (9) Psalms 112:7.

46. Victory

Key Scripture: *"But thanks be to God, which giveth us the victory through our Lord Jesus Christ" (1 Cor. 15:57).*

Key Thought: Faith is the victory that overcomes the world. (See 1 John 5:4.)

Prayer: Yours, O Lord, is the greatness, and the power, and the glory, and the victory, and the majesty, for all that is in the heaven and in the earth is yours. Yours is the kingdom, O Lord, and you are exalted as head above all.[1] Therefore, O God, I thank you, and I praise your glorious name. [2]

Because you are the victory, and you have given me the victory through Jesus Christ my Lord,[3] I am able to be more than a conqueror through Christ who loves me.[4]

For I am persuaded that neither death, nor life, nor angels, nor principalities, nor powers, nor things present, nor things yet to come, nor height, nor depth, nor any other creature shall be able to separate me from your love which is in Christ Jesus, my Lord.[5]

Thank you, Father, for the power of your Word,[6] your Holy Spirit,[7] the blood of Jesus,[8] and the name of Jesus,[9] which you have given to me to make me completely victorious in every area of my life. It is the faith your

Word imparts to me that is my victory, and this faith enables me to overcome the world.[10]

No weapon that is formed against me will ever prosper or succeed.[11] Thank you for always giving me the victory.

References: *(1) 1 Chronicles 29:11; (2) 1 Chronicles 29:13; (3) 1 Corinthians 15:57; (4) Romans 8:37; (5) Romans 8:38-39; (6) Hebrews 4:12; (7) Acts 1:8; (8) Revelation 12:11; (9) Philippians 2:10; (10) 1 John 5:4; (11) Isaiah 54:17.*

47. Walking in the Light

Key Scripture: *"The entrance of thy words giveth light" (Ps. 119:130).*

Key Thought: The Word of God will light your path. (See Ps. 119:105.)

Prayer: Heavenly Father, you are light, and in you there is no darkness at all.[1] You are the Father of lights. With you there is no variation, nor shadow of turning.[2] I desire to walk in your light at all times.

As I walk in your light, Lord God, as you are in the light, I have fellowship with you and other believers, and the blood of Jesus Christ, your Son, cleanses me from all sin.[3]

Father, your Word is a lamp unto my feet and a light unto my path.[4] I will walk in the light of your Word, for the entrance of your Word gives me light.[5]

From this time forward, I will walk as your child of light, for the fruit of the Spirit is in all goodness, righteousness, and truth.[6] As I walk in the light, I will have no fellowship with the unfruitful works of darkness. Rather, I will reprove them and expose them.[7]

References: *(1) 1 John 1:5; (2) James 1:17; (3) 1 John 1:7; (4) Psalms 119:105; (5) Psalms 119:130; (6) Ephesians 5:8-9.*

48. Walking in the Spirit

Key Scripture: *"This I say then, Walk in the Spirit, and ye shall not fulfil the lust of the flesh"* *(Gal. 5:16).*

Key Thought: To be spiritually minded is life and peace. (See Rom. 8:6.)

Prayer: Father, I now invite you to pour your Holy Spirit into every part of my life, to continuously fill me,[1] to comfort me,[2] to teach me,[3] to guide me,[4] to show me things to come,[5] to empower me to witness,[6] to quicken me,[7] to help me in prayer,[8] and to produce His fruit in my life.[9]

Father, you have poured out your Spirit upon all flesh.[10] Fill me now to overflowing with your Spirit.[11] Your love is now pouring into my heart by the Holy Spirit which you have given to me,[12] and His joy is overflowing in my life.[13]

Thank you for your grace which enables me to walk in the Spirit. Your grace and your power keep me from walking in the flesh.[14] Help me to yield myself more and more to the power of your Spirit, Father, because I know that the law of the Spirit of life in Christ Jesus has set me free from the law of sin and death.[15]

Help me to crucify my flesh, Lord, with all its affections and lusts so that I will live and walk in your Spirit at all times. Because your Spirit dwells within me, however, it is now possible for me to keep on walking in your Spirit.[16] Thank you, Father.

As I walk in the Spirit, Father, I am able to enjoy bearing the fruit of the Holy Spirit in all the relationships and responsibilities of my life this day.[17]

I love you, Father, and I know that as your Holy Spirit fills me, He will lead me to walk in the ways of your love.[18]

References: *(1) Ephesians 5:18; (2) John 16:7; (3) John 14:26; (4) Galatians 5:18; (5) John 16:13; (6) Acts 1:8; (7) Romans 8:11; (8) Romans 8:26; (9) Galatians 5:22-23; (10) Acts 2:17-18; (11) Ephesians 5:18; (12) Romans 5:5; (13) 1 Thessalonians 1:6; (14) Galatians 5:16-17; (15) Romans 8:1-2; (16) Galatians 5:25; (17) Galatians 5:22-23; (18) Ephesians 5:2.*

49. Wholeness

Key Scripture: *"For in him dwelleth all the fullness of the Godhead bodily. And ye are complete in him, which is the head of all principality and power" (Col. 2:9-10).*

Key Thought: Wholeness stems from holiness.

Prayer: Father, thank you for your grace which enabled me to receive Jesus Christ as my Lord and Savior. With your help, I will continue to walk in Him.[1] Fulfill my desire to be rooted and built up in Him and established in the faith as I have been taught, with thanksgiving.[2] Fill me with the knowledge of your will, in all wisdom and spiritual understanding, so that I may walk worthy of you, Lord, fully pleasing unto you and fruitful in every good work as I increase in my knowledge of you.[3] Thank you for strengthening me with all might, according to your glorious power, unto all patience and longsuffering with joyfulness.[4]

Father, my heart is filled with gratitude for all you have done for me. You have made me a partaker of the saints' inheritance in your light.[5] You have delivered me from the power of darkness and have translated me into the Kingdom of your dear Son.[6] Through the blood of Jesus, you have provided me with redemption and forgiveness for all my sins.[7] Thank you, Father, for Jesus who is the perfect image of yourself, and He is the first-born of every creature.[8] By Him, all things in heaven and in earth were created. They were created by Him and for Him.[9] Thank you for Jesus, Father.

Your Word proclaims that Jesus is before all things, and by Him all things hold together.[10] He is the Head of the Body, His Church. He is the beginning,[11] as well as the first and the last.[12] He is Alpha and Omega.[13]

I am so thankful, Father that it pleased you to let all fullness dwell in your Son, Jesus.[14] Thank you for His blood which has made peace with you possible and reconciles all things, including myself, to you.[15] Through His great redemption I know I have wholeness. Indeed, I am complete in Him.[16] In every part of my life, Father, I ask you to help me to give Jesus the preeminence in all things.[17]

Thank you for the wholeness you've imparted to me.

References: *(1) Colossians 2:6; (2) Colossians 2:7; (3) Colossians 1:9-10; (4) Colossians 1:11; (5) Colossians 1:12; (6) Colossians 1:13; (7) Colossians 1:14; (8) Colossians 1:15; (9) Colossians 1:16; (10) Colossians 1:17; (11) Colossians 1:18; (12) Revelation 1:11; (13) Revelation 1:11; (14) Colossians 1:19; (15) Colossians 1:20; (16) Colossians 2:10; (17) Colossians 1:18.*

50. Worshiping God

Key Scripture: *"God is a Spirit: and they that worship him must worship him in spirit and in truth" (John 4:24).*

Key Thought: Only God is worthy of worship.

Prayer: You are worthy, O Lord, to receive glory and honor and power, because you have created all things, and for your pleasure they are and were created.[1]

Yours, O Lord, is the greatness, and the power, and the glory, and the victory, and the majesty, for all that is in the heaven and in the earth is yours. Yours is the kingdom, O Lord, and you are exalted as head above all. Both riches and honor come from you, and you reign over all. In your hand is power and might, and in your hand it is to make great and to give strength unto all. Now, therefore, my God, I thank you and I praise your glorious name.[2]

Father, you are seeking true worshipers, who will worship you in spirit and in truth.[3] I will be such a worshiper, because I love you with all my heart, soul, mind, and strength.[4]

Through Christ, therefore, I will offer the sacrifice of praise to you continually, that is, the fruit of my lips, giving thanks to your name.[5]

References: (1) Revelation 4:11; (2) 1 Chronicles 29:12-13; (3) John 4:23; (4) Mark 12:30; (5) Hebrews 13:15.

FAMILY NEEDS

1. The Needs of Your Children

Key Scripture: *"Train up a child in the way he should go: and when he is old, he will not depart from it" (Prov. 22:6).*

Key Thought: Children need models rather than critics.

Prayer: Lord God in heaven, I thank you for the precious children you have given to me. Help me to be a joyful parent to them at all times.[1] My heart is full of thanksgiving and joy when I realize that my children are gifts from you — indeed, they are wonderful rewards from your hands.[2] Help me to always cherish them as an inheritance I have received from you, Father.

Help me to remember, Lord, that my children are not my possessions. They are special people that you have created for your particular purposes. They are fearfully and wonderfully made, Father, and this knowledge causes me to praise you, because I know all your works are marvelous.[3]

Keep me from ever provoking my children to wrath, but help me always to remember your mandate to bring them up in your nurture and admonition, Father.[4]

Keep my children from evil, Lord,[5] and give your angels charge over them.[6] Protect them and lead them in the paths of righteousness for your name's sake.[7] Help my children to remember you in the days of their youth, while the evil days are not near.[8] May they always be examples of what it means to be a true believer in every way.[9]

Bless my children, Lord, in the same way that Jesus blessed the little ones who came to Him.[10] Keep them in the center of your will. Help them to discover your calling in their lives at an early age as they surrender their will to you and learn to trust you for salvation and eternal life.[11]

Thank you for my children, Father.

References: (1) Psalms 113:9; (2) Psalms 127:3; (3) Psalms 139:14; (4) Ephesians 6:4; (5) John 17:15; (6) Psalms 91:11; (7) Psalms 23:3; (8) Ecclesiastes 12:1; (9) 1 Timothy 4:12; (10) Matthew 19:14; (11) John 3:16.

2. When You Desire to Have a Child

Key Scripture: *"Now unto him that is able to do exceeding abundantly above all that we ask or think, according to the power that worketh in us, Unto him be glory in the church by Christ Jesus throughout all ages, world without end. Amen"* (Eph. 3:20-21).

Key Thought: God hears your prayers.

Prayer: Thank you for children, Father. They make life both sweet and challenging. Praise you, Lord, for the ways in which you bless your people. I'm asking you now to bless us with the baby we desire, because I realize that children are an inheritance from you and the fruit of the womb is a reward from your hands.[1]

As you made Sara, who had been barren, into a joyful mother, I express faith to you that you will bless us with a child. Through faith, Sara received the strength she needed to conceive, and your power enabled her to deliver a child when she was past the normal child-bearing age. She trusted in your faithfulness, and I do too, Father.[2]

Help me to keep on believing and to trust you more fully. Protect my mind and heart from any negative words or thoughts. I thank you, Lord, for your promise that you will not let me be confounded.

As arrows are in the hand of a mighty man, so are children of our youth.[3] They bring us happiness, meaning, and joy. I praise you, Father, for every prayer promise of your Word. You assure me that whatever I ask I will receive from you when I keep your commandments and do those things that are pleasing in your sight.[4]

Thank you, Father, for hearing my prayer for a child. I look forward to all you have in store for me.

References: *(1) Psalms 127:3; (2) Hebrews 11:11; (3) Psalms 127:4-5; (4) 1 John 3:22-23.*

3. When Your Child Needs Discipline

Key Scripture: *"Train up a child in the way he should go: and when he is old, he will not depart from it" (Prov. 22:6).*

Key Thought: The best thing to spend on children is your time.

Prayer: Heavenly Father, thank you for the privilege of being a parent. Give me your wisdom[1] so that I will be able to guide and discipline my child in the way that he/she should go. Thank you for your promise which assures me that my child will not depart from my teaching when he/she is older.[2]

Thank you for teaching me your ways;[3] help me to teach your ways to my child, both by word and example. With your help, I will never provoke my child to wrath, Father.[4] Help me to bring him/her up in your nurture and admonition.[5] Always set a watch before my lips, O Lord as I communicate with my child.[6]

Keep me tender-hearted, full of mercy, and forgiving in my relationship with my child.[7] May I always walk in your ways before him/her,[8] for I realize that your way is perfect and your Word is true.[9]

Bless my child with a compliant and responsive attitude. Fill my child with wisdom and understanding so that he/she will walk in your ways throughout his/her life.[10] I pray that my child will always be responsive to your love and direction. May my child always delight in you, Lord, and have the desires of his/her heart fulfilled.[11]

References: *(1) James 1:5-7; (2) Proverbs 22:6; (3) Psalms 25:4; (4) Ephesians 6:4; (5) Ephesians 6:4; (6) Psalms 141:3; (7) Ephesians 4:32; (8) Ephesians 2:10; (9) Psalms 18:30; (10) Ephesians 1:17; (11) Psalms 37:4.*

4. The Needs of Elderly Parents

Key Scripture: *"Even to your old age and gray hairs I am he, I am he who will sustain you. I have made you and I will carry you; I will sustain you and I will rescue you"* (Isa. 46:4, NIV).

Key Thought: We don't have to *be* old when we grow old.

Prayer: Heavenly Father, I thank you for my elderly parents whom I respect and honor with all my heart.[1] Help me to minister to their needs in the power of your Holy Spirit.[2]

Lord God, I pray that they will walk in the full truth of the Gospel of Jesus Christ, and that they will prosper and be in good health as their soul prospers.[3] I pray also that the same Spirit that raised Christ from the dead will be active in them, quickening their mortal bodies, and bringing His life and strength to them.[4]

Keep them close to you, Father, so that they shall still bring forth fruit in their old age, and bless them in every way.[5]

Give them continued longevity and peace, I pray.[6] Help them to trust your faithfulness in all things.[7] Remind them of your great faithfulness in their lives, Father; let them recall that you have never forsaken them.[8]

Keep them conscious of the fact that you will never leave them nor forsake them.[9] Let their hope and joy be in the realization that Jesus Christ will surely return in the near future.[10] Give them the confidence that comes from the knowledge that your goodness and mercy will follow them all the days of their lives, and that they will dwell in your house forever.[11]

Thank you, Father, for hearing and answering my prayers.

References: *(1) Ephesians 6:1-2; (2) Ephesians 5:18; (3) 3 John 2; (4) Romans 8:11; (5) Psalms 92:14; (6) Proverbs 3:2; (7) Psalms 37:25; (8) Isaiah 41:17; (9) Hebrews 13:5; (10) 1 Thessalonians 2:19; (11) Psalms 23:6.*

5. The Needs of Your Family

Key Scripture: *"And if it seem evil unto you to serve the Lord, choose you this day whom ye will serve; whether the gods which your fathers served that were on the other side of the flood, or the gods of the Amorites, in whose land ye dwell: but as for me and my house, we will serve the Lord"* (Josh. 24:15).

Key Thought: "A happy family is but an earlier heaven" (Sir John Bowring).

Prayer: Heavenly Father, you are the one who sets the solitary into families,[1] and you have promised to be a Father to the fatherless.[2] I pray for my family, Lord, that you would ever watch over our comings and goings, and that underneath us we would always find your everlasting arms.[3]

Bless our family, Lord, and keep us safe from all harm.[4] Plant your hedge of protection around us,[5] and let us always dwell in safety.[6] Thank you for blessing our family with all spiritual blessings in heavenly places in Christ.[7]

Help me to remember that our home will be built through wisdom, and by understanding it will be established.[8] By knowledge shall all the chambers of our home be filled with precious and pleasant riches.[9] Thank you, Father.

Your Word, O Lord, declares that the home of the righteous shall be filled with much treasure.[10] In times of wickedness, you have promised that the house of the righteous will stand.[11] Thank you, Father. I believe this promise, and I appropriate it for my home and family.

Because I believe on your Son, the Lord and Savior Jesus Christ, I know that you have saved me, and I claim your promise that you will save my household as well.[12] Thank you, Father, for all your abundant blessings in my life and the lives of my family.

References: *(1) Psalms 68:6; (2) Psalms 68:5; (3) Deuteronomy 33:27; (4) Proverbs 29:25; (5) Job 1:10; (6) Psalms 4:8; (7) Ephesians 1:3; (8) Proverbs 24:3-4; (9) Proverbs 24:4; (10) Proverbs 15:6; (11) Proverbs 12:7; (12) Acts 16:31.*

6. When You Feel You've Been Deserted by Your Loved Ones

Key Scripture: *"And they that know thy name will put their trust in thee: for thou, Lord, hast not forsaken them that seek thee" (Ps. 9:10).*

Key Thought: Our Father is the God who is always there.

Prayer: Heavenly Father, when my loved ones forsake me I know you will be there for me.[1] Thank you for the truth that you will never cast off your people and you will not forsake your inheritance.[2] I praise you for including me in that number, Lord.

I believe the promises of your Word, Father. Therefore, I know you will not let me be forsaken or desolate any longer. This is because you delight in me, Lord, and I will praise you forever.[3] Realizing these precious truths, I cast all my cares upon you, because I know you care for me.[4]

You, O Lord my God, are merciful and I know you will not forsake me.[5] Thank you, Father, for setting your love upon me and delivering me. Indeed, you have set me on high, because I know your name. When I call upon you, Father, you always answer me. Thank you for being with me in times of trouble and for delivering me and honoring me.[6]

All my hope is in you, Father. I will praise you because you are the health of my countenance and you are my God.[7] Because of your promises, I will be strong and of good courage. You always go with me, Father, and I know you will never fail me nor forsake me.[8]

I love you, Lord, and I thank you for loving me.

References: *(1) Psalms 27:10; (2) Psalms 94:14; (3) Isaiah 62:4; (4) 1 Peter 5:7; (5) Deuteronomy 4:31; (6) Psalms 91:14-15; (7) Psalms 43:5; (8) Deuteronomy 31:6.*

7. God's Blessing Upon Your Home

Key Scripture: *"The wicked are overthrown, and are not: but the house of the righteous shall stand" (Prov. 12:7).*

Key Thought: Through wisdom, a home is built. (See Prov. 9:1.)

Prayer: Father, your Word declares to me that a home is built through wisdom, and by understanding it will be established. By knowledge all the chambers of my home will be filled with precious and pleasant riches.[1] Therefore, I ask you for the wisdom, the understanding, and the knowledge your Word promises to me.[2] As for me and my family, we will serve you,[3] and walk continually in the wisdom you have granted to us.[4]

Thank you for all the promises of your Word which declare to me that your blessing will be upon my family and home. I choose to obey you, Father, and in so doing, I know you will command your blessing upon my home.[5] I greatly rejoice in your blessing, Lord, because you are establishing my home.[6] You are prospering,[7] protecting,[8] and blessing[9] my home because of your mercy[10] and your everlasting love.[11]

Father, you have filled my heart with gladness. I am able to sleep peacefully in my home, because you are keeping my home safe.[12] I put my total trust in you, and this gives me tremendous joy. Your blessing and your favor protect me and my home like a shield.[13] Because of this, I know that my home will be blessed and remain standing.[14]

Fill our home with your loving presence.

References: *(1) Proverbs 24:3-4; (2) James 1:5-6; (3) Joshua 24:15; (4) Proverbs 2:6-7; (5) Deuteronomy 28:8; (6) Proverbs 24:3-4; (7) Proverbs 15:6; (8) Psalms 91; (9) Genesis 22:17; (10) Psalms 107:1; (11) Jeremiah 31:3; (12) Psalms 4:7-8; (13) Psalms 5:11-12; (14) Proverbs 12:7.*

8. When You Are Having Marital Problems

Key Scripture: *"Be ye kind one to another, tenderhearted, forgiving one another, even as God for Christ's sake hath forgiven you" (Eph. 4:32).*

Key Thought: "Marriage is our last, best chance to grow up" (Joseph Barth).

Prayer: Heavenly Father, thank you for my spouse and family. Help me to put aside all bitterness, wrath, and anger so that I will be able to work on the issues of my marriage with your help.[1]   I pray for my spouse, _____, right now, and as I do so, I know you are changing my heart. Thank you, Lord.

Thank you for my spouse, Father.   I believe you gave him/her to me, because you did not want me to be alone.[2] Teach us how to communicate better, to be tender-hearted toward each other,[3] and to be submissive to each other.[4]

Help me to do everything I possibly can to develop our marriage into the model you give us in Ephesians 5. Thank you for showing me that our marriage can be a relationship that is like Christ's relationship with His Church.[5] Help me to do my part, Lord.

Thank you for joining me to my spouse as one flesh.[6] Help me to love and respect my spouse at all times.[7]

It is my desire, Father, to serve you. Help me and my spouse to make the conscious choice together to choose to serve you at all times.[8] Lead us to put you and your righteousness first in our lives and in our marriage.[9]

Thank you, Father, for showing me that my spouse and I are heirs together of your grace of life. Show me how to honor my spouse so that my prayers will never be hindered.[10]

Lord, I believe you are at work in my marriage, and I thank you that the troubles of this present time are not worthy to be compared with the glory you are going to reveal to us.[11]

References: *(1) Ephesians 4:31-32; (2) Genesis 2:18; (3) Ephesians 4:32; (4) Ephesians 5:21; (5) Ephesians 5; (6) Ephesians 5:31; (7) 1 Peter 3:7; (8) Joshua 24:15; (9) Matthew 6:33; (10) 1 Peter 3:7; (11) Romans 8:18.*

9. The Needs of Your Marriage

Key Scripture: *"And the Lord God said, It is not good that the man should be alone; I will make him an help meet for him" (Gen. 2:18).*

Key Thought: Each for the other, and both for God.

Prayer: Heavenly Father, thank you for your blessing upon my marriage. You truly have made my spouse and me as one flesh before you.[1] Thank you, Lord, for my marriage partner. Help me always to remember that marriage is an honorable estate and that the marriage bed is undefiled.[2]

We delight in the good favor you've shown to us, Father.[3] Thank you for all the promises of blessing your Word imparts to us, especially for your promise that you will increase us and not diminish us.[4] Help my spouse and me to remember that though we are married to each other, we are betrothed to you, Lord, in righteousness, judgment, lovingkindness, mercy, and faithfulness. Help us to continually walk in your righteousness, judgment, lovingkindness, mercy, and faithfulness, Father.[5]

Show us how to render benevolence toward each other, as your Word commands. Teach us to be mutually submissive, through love, toward each other in the same way that your Son, our Lord and Savior, Jesus Christ, loves His church, the people He gave His very life to redeem. Thank you, Father, for making my spouse and me members of the Body of Christ, of His flesh, and of His bones. Even though this is a great mystery to us, thank you for the example Christ has given to us concerning our marriage. Help us to live up to all your expectations, Father, through love and reverence toward each other.[6]

We realize, Lord, that we are heirs together of the grace of life. Thank you, Lord. This wonderful knowledge leads me to realize that our prayers will never be hindered.[7]

Thank you for my marriage and my spouse. Through your Holy Spirit, Father, I ask you to bless my marriage and my spouse with your love, peace, and joy.[8]

References: *(1) Genesis 2:24; (2) Hebrews 13:4; (3) Proverbs 18:20-24; (4) Jeremiah 29:6; (5) Hosea 2:19-20; (6) Ephesians 5:22-33; (7) 1 Peter 3:7; (8) Galatians 5:22-23.*

10. When a New Baby Is Born

Key Scripture: *"For this child I prayed; and the Lord hath given me my petition which I asked of him: Therefore also I have lent him to the Lord; as long as he liveth he shall be lent to the Lord" (1 Sam. 1:27-28).*

Key Thought: A baby is a bundle of divine potential.

Prayer: Heavenly Father, I come to you now with a heart filled with gratitude and adoration on the occasion of the birth of my child: _____. Thank you for my child.

I recognize that this child is an inheritance I have received from you, Father. This child is a reward from your hands.[1] Thank you, Father.

Let my child be filled with wisdom throughout his/her life, Lord. This will make my heart and your heart glad.[2] Give my child wisdom, Father, for I know this will be a source of great joy for him and me.[3] Teach my child that true wisdom comes from honoring you,[4] Father, and grant him/her a heart that always desires your wisdom, understanding, and knowledge.[5]

As arrows are in the hand of a mighty man, so are the children of one's youth. Thank you for this child, Father, for I am truly

happy and blessed.[6] Teach _____
_____to love you, obey you, and to
honor his/her elders throughout his/her life.[7]
In so doing, Lord, I know it will be well with
him/her, and you will cause his/her days to
be long on the earth.[8] Thank you for all the
precious promises of your Word, Father.

I dedicate my child to you, Father, and I
ask you to watch over him/her, and to bring
him/her to a saving knowledge of Jesus Christ.[9]

Bless my child abundantly in every way.

References: *(1) Psalms 127:3; (2) Proverbs
15:20; (3) Proverbs 23:24; (4) Psalms 111:10;
(5) Proverbs 2:6; (6) Psalms 127:4-5; (7) Ephesians
6:1; (8) Ephesians 6:3; (9) Romans 10:17.*

11. When You Need Parental Wisdom

Key Scripture: *"For the Lord giveth wisdom: out of his mouth cometh knowledge and understanding"* *(Prov. 2:6).*

Key Thought: Wisdom has God's thoughts on any matter.

Prayer: Dear Lord, my loving Father, I ask you now for the wisdom I need to be the most effective parent possible. Thank you for giving your wisdom to me.[1] Help me at all times to raise my child in your nurture and admonition.[2]

I thank you for your Word which imparts wisdom unto me. I enter your presence with trust, Father, knowing that you are giving me your wisdom.[3] Let your wisdom so work in me that I will always reflect its qualities of purity, peace, gentleness, and mercy in my relationships with my child and others.[4]

With you, Lord, I have strength and wisdom.[5] Let my mouth speak your wisdom, Lord, because of the righteousness you have imparted unto me.[6] In the hidden parts of my life, make me to know wisdom.[7] Lord, help me to apply my heart unto your wisdom at all times.[8]

Give my child an understanding heart that openly responds to the wisdom and direction he/she receives,[9] and is responsive and obedient to all your will.[10]

As a parent under your authority, Father, I will walk in your Word. As I do so, I receive your knowledge, instruction, wisdom, and understanding.[11] Fill both me and my child with the knowledge of your will in all wisdom and spiritual understanding. I desire to walk worthy of you, Lord God, unto all pleasing, and to be fruitful in every good work, increasing in the knowledge of your ways at all times.[12]

Thank you for fulfilling your promise of wisdom to me Lord God.

References: *(1) James 1:5-7; (2) Ephesians 6:4; (3) 2 Chronicles 1:10; (4) James 3:15-17; (5) Job 12:13; (6) Psalms 37:30; (7) Psalms 51:6; (8) Psalms 90:12; (9) 1 Kings 3:9; (10) Proverbs 3:1; (11) 2 Chronicles 1:10; (12) Colossians 1:9-11.*

12. When You Need God's
Help With Parenting

Key Scripture: *"Train up a child in the way he should go: and when he is old, he will not depart from it" (Prov. 22:6).*

Key Thought: Parenting is a ministry ordained of God.

Prayer: Heavenly Father, I treasure my children as being an heritage and a reward from you. As arrows are in the hands of a mighty man, so are my children to me. Thank you for blessing me with my children, and for the happiness they bring to me.[1] I gladly commit myself, Lord, to the important responsibility of training my children in the way that they should go. I know that if I will do this faithfully, my children will not depart from my training and your guidance when they are older.[2]

Father-God, thank you for being the perfect example of Fatherhood,[3] and thank you for your Word which guides me as a parent at all times.[4] Teach me how to be the best possible parent I can be, making sure that my children exhibit self-control, respect, and dignity at all times. With your help, Father, I will be able to lead them without ever provoking them.[5] Help me to be fair with my children and to understand them, even as you understand me. Give me your wisdom at all times,[6] Father, so that I will be the kind of parent you desire for me to be.

As a parent, Lord, I trust in you with all my heart. I will avoid leaning to my own understanding. In all my ways I acknowledge you, and I know you are directing, and will direct, my paths.[7] Thank you, Father.

References: *(1) Psalms 127:3-5; (2) Proverbs 22:6; (3) Isaiah 63:16; (4) Psalms 119:105; (5) Ephesians 6:4; (6) James 1:5-7; (7) Proverbs 3:5-6.*

13. Protection for Your Home and Family

Key Scripture: *"But the Lord is faithful, who shall stablish you, and keep you from evil"* (2 Thess. 3:3).

Key Thought: The eternal God is your refuge. (See Deut. 33:27.)

Prayer: Lord God Almighty, thank you for your faithfulness. I know that I can depend on you to establish my home and my family, and to keep us from all evil.[1] Eternal God, you are our refuge, and your everlasting arms are underneath us at all times.[2] Let your ministering angels watch over every member of my family.[3] Thank you for your ministering angels which encamp around me and my family because we love you, and thank you for delivering us from all evil.[4] Be a protecting wall of fire around us, O God, and be glorious in our midst.[5]

You are our Shepherd, O Lord. Your rod and your staff comfort us. You set a table before us in the presence of our enemies, and we are safe. Surely goodness and mercy will follow us all the days of our lives, and we will dwell in your house forever.[6]

Your eyes are always watching over us, and your ears are always open to our prayers.[7] You, O Lord, are our shield, our glory, and the lifter of our heads.[8]

Lord God, you are our rock, and our fortress. You are our Deliverer, our God, our strength, and in you we place our complete trust. You are our buckler, and the horn of our salvation, and you are our high tower [9] in which we find our safety.[10]

Thank you for your protection, Father.

References: (1) 2 Thessalonians 3:3; (2) Deuteronomy 33:27; (3) Hebrews 1:13-14; (4) Psalms 34:7; (5) Zechariah 2:5; (6) Psalms 23; (7) 1 Peter 3:12; (8) Psalms 3:3; (9) Psalms 18:2; (10) Proverbs 18:10.

14. The Salvation of a Loved One

Key Scripture: *"That if thou shalt confess with thy mouth the Lord Jesus, and shalt believe in thine heart that God hath raised him from the dead, thou shalt be saved. For with the heart man believeth unto righteousness; and with the mouth confession is made unto salvation" (Rom. 10:9-10).*

Key Thought: God wants everyone to receive eternal life. (See John 3:16.)

Prayer: Dear God, thank you for all your promises. Your Word assures me that you are not willing for anyone to perish, because you want everyone to come to repentance.[1] I claim this promise now in behalf of my loved one: _____. Draw him/her to yourself through the power of your Holy Spirit.[2]

Give _____ a spirit of wisdom and revelation in the knowledge of you, so that the eyes of his/her understanding will be enlightened, and he/she will know the hope to which you have called him/her.[3]

Help _____ to see his/her need for repentance. You are near, Lord, to all who have a broken heart, and you save those who have a contrite spirit.[4] Bring brokenness to _____ so that he/she will see his/her need for you.

Thank you for your promise, Father, that whosoever will call upon your name shall be saved.[5] So work in my loved one's life that he/she will want to call upon your name.[6]

Right now, Father, on the authority of your Word,[7] in the name of Jesus,[8] and by the precious blood of Christ,[9] I pray that every plan and strategy of the enemy in _____ _____'s life be stopped and rendered of no effect. Let every plan of the powers of darkness against _____'s life fail.[10]

Send believers who will proclaim the gospel to _____ in the power of your Holy Spirit,[11] so that his/her eyes will be opened and that he/she will turn from darkness to light.[12]

Thank you for giving him/her eternal life with you, Father.

References: *(1) 2 Peter 3:9; (2) 1 Corinthians 12:3; (3) Ephesians 1:17-18; (4) Psalms 34:18; (5) Acts 2:21; (6) Romans 10:13; (7) Isaiah 55:11; (8) Philippians 2:10; (9) 1 Peter 1:19-21; (10) Ephesians 6:12; (11) Acts 1:8; (12) Acts 26:18.*

15. A Single Believer Who
Desires to Be Married

Key Scripture: *"Therefore shall a man leave his father and mother, and shall cleave unto his wife: and they shall be one flesh" (Gen. 2:24).*

Key Thought: God promises to give you the desires of your heart. (See Ps. 37:4.)

Prayer: Dear Lord God, I trust you with all my heart as I seek your will regarding marriage. The desire of my heart is to be married to the partner you have selected for me. As I trust in you, and commit my way unto you, I know you will direct my paths.[1] Thank you, Father.

Knowing that you care for me, I give you all my cares and concerns about marriage.[2] I thank you for taking them away from me as I yield them to you.

Now I ask you to work in the life of my future mate so that he/she will know your will and be prepared for marriage. I pray for myself and my future mate, asking that we both will be transformed by the renewing of our minds so that we both will walk in your good, acceptable, and perfect will concerning our marriage.[3]

Help me always to be wise with regard to understanding your will as it is revealed in your holy Word.[4] As I learn to seek first your kingdom and your righteousness, I know that you will take care of everything I am concerned about, including my desire to be married.[5]

I believe, Lord God, that all things do work together for good in my life because I love you and you have called me to your purpose.[6]

Thank you, Father, for blessing my life in so many ways.

References: (1) Proverbs 3:5-6; (2) 1 Peter 5:7; (3) Romans 12:1-2; (4) Ephesians 5:17; (5) Matthew 6:33; (6) Romans 8:28.

16. The Needs of a Single Parent

Key Scripture: *"I will instruct thee and teach thee in the way which thou shalt go: I will guide thee with mine eye" (Ps. 32:8).*

Key Thought: The greatest of all parents is helping you.

Prayer: Dear God, your Word assures me that no evil will befall me or my children, and that the angels of heaven will keep us in all our ways. I claim this promise especially for my children, and I know that angelic protection will bear them up and keep them safe.[1] Thank you, Father.

Guide me in my parenting, Lord.[2] I receive your words, and I hide your commands in my heart. As I do this, my heart inclines to your wisdom, and I apply my heart to your understanding. I cry for your knowledge, and I lift up my voice for understanding. I seek your wisdom as silver, and I search for your wisdom as I would search for a hidden treasure. Thank you, Father, for enabling me to understand the reverential fear of you, and for helping me to know you, for you have given me wisdom, and from your mouth I receive knowledge and understanding.[3]

Lord God, my children are so important to me. I realize that they are a wonderful heritage you have given to me. My precious children are a reward from your hands.[4] Help me to love my children the way they need to be loved.[5] Lord, you have promised to be a parent to my children and to me.[6] Thank you, Father. I am so grateful that you are willing to share the responsibilities of parenting with me, and you are showing me how to be an effective parent at all times, through your guidance.

References: *(1) Psalms 91:10-11; (2) Psalms 32:8; (3) Proverbs 2:1-6; (4) Psalms 127:3; (5) Ephesians 5:2; (6) Psalms 68:5.*

17. The Needs of Your Soon-to-be-Born Child

Key Scripture: *"For thou hast possessed my reins: thou hast covered me in my mother's womb. I will praise thee; for I am fearfully and wonderfully made: marvellous are thy works; and that my soul knoweth right well" (Ps. 139:13-14).*

Key Thought: Every child is a blessing from God.

Prayer: Lord God, I thank you for the gift of life you have imparted to the precious person you are creating even now. It is an honor for me to welcome our soon-to-be-born baby into our home and family. I praise you, Father, for the child you are giving to us.[1] This is a joyous experience, and indeed it is such a privilege for me.

May the womb in which the baby rests be covered with your love.[2] Give this child an awareness of your presence.[3] I pray that he/she will always know that you are with him/her,[4] and ever experience the fullness of joy that comes from knowing you.[5] May he/she always be sensitive to your Spirit, and walk in your truth.[6] As he/she learns to bond together with us (his/her parents), may he/she also learn to bond with you, Father,[7] as we walk in your ways[8] and teach your truths to him/her.[9]

Father, I thank you that you see my/our baby's substance even as he/she is being made in secret.[10]   You know him/her intimately. Begin even now, Lord, to call him/her and to prepare his/her heart to respond to you.[11] Grant health, strength, and vitality to this precious child as you continue to form him/her in the womb.[12]

Dear Lord, let the birthing process go smoothly,[13] and may it be a safe[14] and peaceful[15] experience. I pray that you will lead him/her to trust in you at all times.[16] May he/she be cast upon you from the womb, and know you as his/her God.[17]

Thank you, Father, for this precious child.

References: (1) Psalms 139:14; (2) Psalms 139:13; (3) Luke 1:41; (4) Psalms 139:7; (5) Psalms 16:11; (6) John 16:13; (7) 2 Corinthians 6:16; (8) Deuteronomy 5:33; (9) Deuteronomy 11:18-19; (10) Psalms 139:15; (11) Isaiah 49:1; (12) Isaiah 44:2; (13) 1 Timothy 2:15; (14) Psalms 4:8; (15) Psalms 29:11; (16) Psalms 22:9; (17) Psalms 22:10.

18. The Needs of Your Teenager

Key Scripture: *"Wherewithal shall a young man cleanse his way? by taking heed thereto according to thy word. With my whole heart have I sought thee: O let me not wander from thy commandments. Thy word have I hid in mine heart, that I might not sin against thee"* (Ps. 119:9-11).

Key Thought: Cherish your teenager for whom he or she is, not for whom you want him/her to become.

Prayer: Dear Father in heaven, I come to you now in behalf of my teenager, _____ _____. He/she needs your unfailing love,[1] your wisdom,[2] and your guidance.[3] Thank you for your willingness to supply all his/her needs according to your riches in glory.[4] Lord, supply those needs in the power of your might.[5]

Keep and protect him/her from the evil one.[6] Convict _____ of his/her need for you at all times. Draw him/her to abundant life in you.[7] How I praise and thank you, Father, that you have a plan and a purpose for his/her life.[8] Reveal your will to him/her.[9]

Help _____ to honor and remember you in the days of his/her youth, before the days of trouble come as the years go by.[10] Thank you, Lord, for being the Guide

of our youths.[11] I pray for young people in general, and for my teenager, _____
_____, in particular, that they would find you early and be set free from the prevailing philosophies and behaviors of our day.[12]

Father, may _____
always grow up in you in all things.[13] Help him/her to learn your ways,[14] because your ways are perfect and your Word is true.[15] Lead him/her in the paths of righteousness for your name's sake.[16] May he/she always remember that fearing (respecting, reverencing) you is the beginning of all wisdom.[17]

Bless him/her so that he/she will always be spiritually stalwart,[18] mentally alert, and physically healthy.[19]

References: (1) 1 John 4:16; (2) 2 Chronicles 1:10; (3) Psalms 32:8; (4) Philippians 4:19; (5) Revelation 7:12; (6) Matthew 6:13; (7) John 10:10; (8) Jeremiah 29:11; (9) Psalms 40:8; (10) Ecclesiastes 12:1; (11) Jeremiah 3:4; (12) Colossians 2:8; (13) Ephesians 4:15; (14) Isaiah 2:3; (15) Psalms 18:30; (16) Psalms 23:3; (17) Psalms 111:10; (18) Ephesians 6:10; (19) 3 John 2.

19. The Needs of a Troubled Son or Daughter

Key Scripture: *"Wherewithal shall a young man cleanse his way? by taking heed thereto according to thy word. With my whole heart have I sought thee: O let me not wander from thy commandments. Thy word have I hid in mine heart, that I might not sin against thee" (Ps. 119:9-11).*

Key Thought: God hears your prayers and loves your child.

Prayer: Lord God, my child, _____
_____, is having trouble with _____. I know you care about every aspect of our lives, and because you do, I freely cast all my cares upon you.[1] I pray that my son/daughter will learn to search for you with all his/her heart. Remind him/her of the need to follow your commandments,[2] and to obey his/her parents.[3] Shield and protect him/her from the evil one.[4] Let all strategies and schemes of the enemy against his/her life be stopped, now and forever, in the name of Jesus.[5] Convict _____ of his/her need to draw close to you.[6] Help my child to clearly see the plan and purpose you have for his/her life.[7]

Turn _____'s heart toward you and toward me, Lord, and help me to keep my heart right toward him/her.[8] Many are overwhelmed by the difficult times in the world today, but you, Lord, are more powerful than any difficulty or trouble.[9]

Turn any disobedience in _____
_____'s heart and life to the wisdom of the just. Give him/her an understanding heart that openly responds to the wisdom and direction he/she receives,[10] so that he/she will become responsive and obedient to all your will.[11]

As a parent under your authority, Father, I will walk in your Word. As I do so, I receive your knowledge, instruction, wisdom, and understanding. Fill both me and my child with the knowledge of your will in all wisdom and spiritual understanding. I desire to walk worthy of you, Lord God, unto all pleasing, and to be fruitful in every good work, increasing in the knowledge of you at all times.[12] Thank you for fulfilling your promise of wisdom to me, Lord God.

Thank you for hearing and answering my prayer, Father.

References: *(1) 1 Peter 5:7; (2) Psalms 119:9; (3) Ephesians 6:1; (4) Matthew 6:13; (5) Ephesians 6:11; (6) James 4:8; (7) Jeremiah 29:11; (8) Malachi 4:5-6; (9) 1 Peter 1:5; (10) 1 Kings 3:9; (11) Proverbs 3:1; (12) Colossians 1:9-11.*

20. When You Are Widowed

Key Scripture: *"For thy Maker is thine husband; the Lord of hosts is his name; and thy Redeemer the Holy One of Israel; The God of the whole earth shall he be called" (Isa. 54:5).*

Key Thought: "Nothing can fill the gap when we are away from those we love, and it would be wrong to try and find anything. We must simply hold out and win through. That sounds very hard at first, but at the same time it is a great consolation, since leaving the gap unfilled preserves the bonds between us" (Dietrich Bonhoeffer).

Prayer: Heavenly Father, thank you for your willingness to be my husband.[1] Thank you for the presence of your Holy Spirit, who is my ever-present Comforter. I experience your love and your comfort as I pray.[2] Thank you for healing my broken heart, and for binding up all my wounds.[3]

You are my protector and defender, holy Father.[4] Therefore, I offer the sacrifice of praise to you continually. I give you the fruit of my lips.[5] Your love and your justice give me hope.[6] Thank you for meeting all my needs according to your riches in glory through Christ Jesus.[7]

Lord, you promise to establish my borders,[8] and to me this means that you will always provide a place for me. Thank you, Father. Your blessing in my life causes my heart to sing with joy.[9]

Thank you for preserving me and relieving me of all anxieties.[10] I trust in you, Lord.[11] Teach me to trust in you with all my heart so as to not ever lean unto my own understanding. In all my ways, Father, I will acknowledge you and I know you will direct my paths.[12]

Thank you for being with me during my widowhood, Father.

References: (1) Isaiah 54:5; (2) John 14:16-18; (3) Psalms 147:3; (4) Psalms 68:5; (5) Hebrews 13:15; (6) Deuteronomy 10:18; (7) Philippians 4:19; (8) Proverbs 15:25; (9) Job 29:13; (10) Psalms 146:9; (11) Jeremiah 49:11; (12) Proverbs 3:5-6.

PERSONAL NEEDS

1. Freedom From Addictions

Key Scripture: *"Stand fast therefore in the liberty wherewith Christ hath made us free, and be not entangled again with the yoke of bondage"* *(Gal. 5:1).*

Key Thought: God is more powerful than any addiction.

Prayer: Heavenly Father, I battle the addiction to _____ in my life. I believe you are more powerful than any addiction, and I believe you are able to deliver me.

You have revealed your truth to me through your Word,[1] and I believe your promise which tells me that I shall know the truth, and the truth will make me free.[2] I also believe that when Jesus Christ sets me free I shall be free indeed.[3] Therefore, I seek your deliverance, and I express faith to you that you will bring it to pass in my life now, as I pray.

Father, I realize my addiction is a sin, and I confess it to you now. Thank you for your promise that assures me that when I confess my sins you are faithful and just to forgive me of my sins, and to cleanse me of all unrighteousness.[4] I receive your forgiveness and cleansing now as I repent of my sinful addiction. Lord God, I will stand fast in the liberty wherewith Christ has set me free, and

I will never again be entangled with the yoke of bondage that addiction brings.[5]

I praise you, Father, that the law of the spirit of life in Christ Jesus has made me free from the law of sin and death.[6] I surrender my life to you entirely, because you have freed me from my sin. From now on, I will be your servant, O God, and I will enjoy your fruit in my life unto holiness, and I know I have already received everlasting life.[7] Thank you, Father.

Thank you for giving me continuing power to tread on serpents and scorpions, and over all the power of the enemy. I now know that nothing shall by any means hurt me.[8] I also know that no weapon that is formed against me shall prosper, because this is my heritage as your servant.[9] Thank you, Father, for complete and total deliverance and freedom from the addiction that used to come between me and you.

References: *(1) John 17:17; (2) John 8:32; (3) John 8:36; (4) 1 John 1:9; (5) Galatians 5:1; (6) Romans 8:2; (7) Romans 6:22; (8) Luke 10:19; (9) Isaiah 54:17.*

2. When You Are Angry

Key Scripture: *"But now ye also put off all these; anger, wrath, malice, blasphemy, filthy communication out of your mouth" (Col. 3:8).*

Key Thought: Anger is a symptom of hurt or frustration. Take your anger to your heavenly Father who understands all things.

Prayer: Heavenly Father, the hurts I've received and the frustrations I feel have caused anger to develop in my life. I bring my anger to you now, and I ask you to replace it with your healing love. You are the Healer of all my inner hurts, frustrations, wounds, and disappointments.[1] Thank you, Lord, for your nurturing in my life.

Father, I thank you for Jesus who is my High Priest. Though He was tempted in all the ways that I've been tempted, He remained without sin, but I know He understands my anger and I believe He will lead me to freedom from its torment in my life.[2]

Lord God, you are full of mercy and grace.[3] I ask you to apply your mercy and grace to the hurts I've received. Please let your Balm of Gilead heal each one.[4] Lord, thank you for inviting me to cast all my cares upon you.[5] I do so now by surrendering my frustrations, hurts, and cares to you. Help me to maintain an attitude of kindness, mercy, and patience toward others.[6] Help me, also, to forsake worrying, judging, and criticizing others, which lead to frustrations and anger.[7]

Teach me to forgive those who hurt me at all times.[8] Help me always to deal with anger in positive, constructive ways. With your help, Lord, I will never let the sun go down on my wrath again.[9] It is my heart-felt desire to always follow your perfect way and will in all things, and to pursue the most excellent way of all — the way of love.[10]

Thank you for lifting the burden of anger from me.

Through your guidance and leadership in my life, I know I will learn to cease from anger and to forsake all wrath.[11] I respond to your love, dear Father, and as I do so, the anger I was feeling is fading away.[12] Thank you so much.

References: *(1) Exodus 15:26; (2) Hebrews 4:15; (3) Psalms 86:5; (4) Jeremiah 8:22; (5) 1 Peter 5:7; (6) Ephesians 4:31-32; (7) Matthew 7:1-5; (8) Colossians 3:13; (9) Ephesians 4:26; (10) 1 Corinthians 12:31; (11) Psalms 37:8; (12) 1 John 4:10.*

3. When You Are Too Busy

Key Scripture: *"For thus saith the Lord God, the Holy One of Israel; In returning and rest shall ye be saved; in quietness and in confidence shall be your strength"* (Isa. 30:15).

Key Thought: "At supper, when you pour the milk, you fill one glass at a time. In your daily affairs, you have to learn to fill each minute at a time, otherwise some minutes will overflow while others remain empty" (Michael Quoist).

Prayer: Heavenly Father, I thank you that you are never too busy for me. In fact, you are my refuge and strength. You are my very present help in times of busy-ness and trouble.[1] Your Son, my Lord and Savior, Jesus Christ, reminds me to come unto Him when I labor and feel overburdened because He will give me rest. I thank you, Father, that His yoke is easy and His burden is light.[2]

Lord, help me to keep my mind stayed on you at all times, because I know this will bring me into your perfect peace. I seek your guidance, Lord God, to help me arrange my priorities properly. Guide me,[3] and help me to think your thoughts as I let the mind of Christ have its rightful authority in my life.[4] I trust you, Father.[5] Because you are my God and my Deliverer, I will not let my heart be either troubled or afraid. This is possible only because Jesus has given me His peace.[6] Thank you, Father.

I praise you, Lord, that you have ordained peace for me, and that you have wrought all your works in my life.[7] Therefore, during this time of busy-ness in my life I will not worry. Instead, I will let all my requests be made known unto you through prayer, with thanksgiving. Even as I pray, Lord, you are giving me your great peace — a peace that surpasses all understanding. Thank you for keeping my heart and mind through Christ Jesus.[8]

I love your Word, Father, and this brings great peace to my soul. Because of your Word, I know nothing shall be able to offend me during this busy season in my life.[9] Lord, I will approach all my responsibilities from a spiritual perspective rather than a carnal mind, because I know that to be spiritually minded is life and peace.[10] Thank you, Lord.

References: (1) Psalms 46:1; (2) Matthew 11:28; (3) Psalms 32:8; (4) Philippians 2:5; (5) Isaiah 26:3; (6) John 14:27; (7) Isaiah 26:12; (8) Philippians 4:6-7; (9) Psalms 119:165; (10) Romans 8:6.

4. When You Need Comfort

Key Scripture: *"I will not leave you comfortless: I will come to you"* (John 14:18).

Key Thought: "I know that my Redeemer lives: What comfort this sweet sentence gives!" (Samuel Medley).

Prayer: Heavenly Father, I bless you because I know you are the Father of my Lord and Savior, Jesus Christ. You are the Father of mercies, and you are the God of all comfort. Thank you for comforting me in all the tribulations and losses I've experienced. I know that the lessons I've learned are invaluable, because you've taught me how to bring comfort to others in the same way you've comforted me.[1] Thank you, Lord.

Your Word is my treasure, Father.   It promises me that you will always be with me, even if I have to pass through flood waters and raging waves. You, Lord, enable me to go through the fires of temptation without being burned.[2] Thank you for loving me so much and for giving me an everlasting consolation and good hope through your grace. How I praise you, Father, that even now you are comforting my heart and establishing me in every good work and word.[3]

Your   Holy   Spirit,   Father,   is   the Comforter in my life.[4] He is always with me, even when I have to walk through the valley of the shadow of death.[5]

Your Word, dear Father, comforts me in my time of affliction. In fact, your Word brings life to me.[6]

Therefore, Lord, as one of your redeemed, I come with singing into your presence, because I know that your everlasting joy is upon my head. I know you will give me gladness and joy, and I thank you that all sorrow and mourning shall flee away.[7] The realization that you are always here with me gives me great peace and comfort.

Thank you for your comforting presence in my life, Father.

References: *(1) 2 Corinthians 1:3-4; (2) Isaiah 43:2; (3) 2 Thessalonians 2:16-17; (4) John 14:16; (5) Psalms 23:4; (6) Psalms 119:50; (7) Isaiah 51:11.*

5. When You Need Confidence

Key Scripture: *"Being confident of this very thing, that he which hath begun a good work in you will perform it until the day of Jesus Christ"* (Phil. 1:6).

Key Thought: A lack of confidence is a lack of faith.

Prayer: Dear Father, I thank you for the fact that I can do all things through Christ because I know He will always strengthen me.[1] This certainty of my faith gives me great confidence in you. With your help, therefore, I will not cast my confidence away. Instead, I will patiently await the fulfillment of your promises as I endeavor to do your will.[2]

I will follow the example of those, who through faith and patience, inherit your promises, Father.[3]

Lord, your Word gives me the confidence that I need. It teaches me that you will continue your workmanship in my life. Indeed, I know you will perform your will and your work in my life until the day of Jesus Christ.[4] Thank you, Father.

The confidence I have in you, Lord, reminds me that you will hear me when I pray according to your will. And just knowing that you are listening gives me great confidence, Father. It builds my faith in you so that I know you will answer my prayers.[5] Bless you, Lord.

You are my confidence, Lord, and I know you will always protect me.[6] Through your Son, my Lord and Savior Jesus Christ, I have complete confidence and boldness as I pray.[7] Thank you for delivering me from all condemnation, Father. This freedom gives me great confidence in you.[8]

You have given me the ability, Lord,[9] to do all things through Christ who strengthens me.[10] Thank you for the confidence this knowledge brings to me.

References: *(1) Philippians 4:13; (2) Hebrews 10:35-36; (3) Hebrews 6:12; (4) Philippians 1:6; (5) 1 John 5:14-15; (6) Proverbs 3:26; (7) Ephesians 3:12; (8) Romans 8:1; (9) 1 Peter 4:11; (10) Philippians 4:13.*

6. When You Feel Confused

Key Scripture: *"For God is not the author of confusion, but of peace, as in all churches of the saints" (1 Cor. 14:33).*

Key Thought: The author of confusion is an enemy of your soul.

Prayer: Heavenly Father, I thank you for the fact that you are not the author of confusion in my life,[1] and because of you I never have to be confused. I praise you for not giving me a spirit of fear; instead, you have given me a spirit of power, love, and a sound mind.[2] Thank you, Lord.

Through your grace, I will trust in you with all my heart, and I will not lean toward my own understanding. In all my ways, Lord, I will acknowledge you and I know you will direct my paths.[3] Praise you, Father.

Teach me to love your law. As I do so, I know I will have great peace in my life instead of confusion.[4] Help me, Father. With your help I know I will not be confused any longer. Your help enables me to set my face like a flint, and I know I shall not be ashamed.[5] Thank you, Father.

You have invited me to cast my burdens upon you, Lord; therefore, I cast my burden of confusion upon you, realizing that you will sustain me. I thank you, Father, for always sustaining me. I know you will never permit me to be swayed from the peace I have in you.[6]

Thank you for your peace which surpasses all understanding. It has taken away the confusion I was experiencing and I know your peace will keep my heart and mind through Christ Jesus.[7]

Thank you for setting me free from confusion, Father.

References: *(1) 1 Corinthians 14:33; (2) 2 Timothy 1:7; (3) Proverbs 3:5-6; (4) Psalms 119:165; (5) Isaiah 50:7; (6) Psalms 55:22; (7) Philippians 4:7.*

7. When You Need Courage

Key Scripture: *"O love the Lord, all ye his saints: for the Lord preserveth the faithful, . . . Be of good courage, and he shall strengthen your heart, all ye that hope in the Lord"* (Ps. 31:23-24).

Key Thought: God always gives us the courage to face life's circumstances, and to make positive changes.

Prayer: Lord, I hope in you and I place my complete and unswerving trust in you.[1] Thank you for giving me the courage to always be strong.[2] Through the courage you are imparting to me I know you will make me swifter than an eagle and stronger than a lion.[3] Thank you for this promise and for all the promises of your Word, Father.

You are the strength of my life; therefore, I will fear no one and no situation that might appear to rise against me.[4] I thank you for the fact that no weapon which is formed against me will ever prosper.[5] Be with me, Lord, and enable me to become a mighty servant of valor in the same way that you empowered Gideon.[6]

Thank you for your promise that I will be strong in you and in the power of your might.[7] Thank you for replacing all fear with your courage. Because of your strength at work in my life, Lord, I will not fear. I know it is your good pleasure to give me your kingdom.[8] Knowing that you are always with me, I am now able to mock at fear and never to walk in fear again.[9]

Encourage me, Lord, as I seek your face and stand upon the promises of your Word. Your Word is truth, and you are my mighty buckler because I trust in you.[10] Thank you for courage, Father.

References: (1) Psalms 7:1; (2) 1 Samuel 4:9; (3) 2 Samuel 1:23; (4) Ezekiel 2:6; (5) Isaiah 54:17; (6) Judges 6:12; (7) Ephesians 6:10; (8) Luke 12:32; (9) Job 39:22; (10) 2 Samuel 22:31.

8. When You Are Depressed

Key Scripture: *"Why art thou cast down, O my soul? and why art thou disquieted within me? hope in God: for I shall yet praise him, who is the health of my countenance, and my God" (Ps. 43:5).*

Key Thought: Hope renewed brings freedom and life.

Prayer: Lord, I thank you for being my Shepherd. Even when I am called upon to walk through the valley of the shadow of death, I will fear no evil; for you are always with me. Your rod and your staff bring comfort to me.[1]

You are the God of all hope, Father, [2] and I will find my hope in you.[3] Simply expressing this to you in prayer lifts the hopelessness I've been feeling. Thank you, Lord God.

I confess the depression I'm experiencing to you, Lord. In so doing, I express my desire to forsake it and to put it behind me forever. Thank you for lifting me from the miry clay and setting my feet upon the solid confidence of your Word.[4] With your help, I will not give in to anger and depression any longer. Instead, I make the commitment to hope and trust implicitly in you.

Lord, through your grace I will trust in you with all my heart, and I will endeavor to never lean unto my own understanding again. In all my ways I will acknowledge you, and I know you will direct my paths.[5]

You are the God of my strength, Father. There is never a reason for me to mourn or to be depressed because of the enemy's oppression. Instead of succumbing to depression, Lord, I will go to you because you are my exceeding joy. Setting my will toward you, Father, I will praise you at all times.[6]

Through faith in your Word, I thank you for setting me free from depression.

References: *(1) Psalms 23; (2) Romans 15:13; (3) Psalms 33:22; (4) Psalms 40:2; (5) Proverbs 3:5-6; (6) Psalms 43:2-4.*

9. When You Feel Discouraged

Key Scripture: *"Let not your heart be troubled: ye believe in God, believe also in me" (John 14:1).*

Key Thought: "He [God] has appointed seasons of refreshment, and you shall find he does not forget you. Above all, keep close to the throne of grace. If we seem to get no good by attempting to draw near him, we may be sure we shall get none by keeping away from him" (John Newton).

Prayer: Thank you, Father, for the trial of my faith which I recognize to be more precious than that of gold.[1] Through prayer I know I am able to rise out of my discouragement. Therefore, in everything (including these troubling circumstances), by prayer and supplication with thanksgiving, I will let my requests be made unto you. Father, I seek your peace and encouragement, because I know your peace surpasses all understanding, and it will keep my heart and mind through Christ Jesus.[2] Thank you, Father.

Though I walk in the midst of trouble and discouragement, I know you will revive me, Lord. I humbly beseech you to stretch forth your hand against the wrath of my enemies, and I know your right hand will save me.[3] Thank you, Lord.

Through your grace, I refuse to cast away the confidence you've imparted to me, Father.[4] I know that you will continue your workmanship in my life until Jesus returns.[5] In place of my discouragement, as I pray, I sense you are giving me courage. I receive your strength, Lord, as I continue to hope in you.[6]

Teach me your way, O Lord, and lead me in a plain path. I wait upon you with the good courage you're imparting to me. Thank you for strengthening my heart.[7]

You, Lord, are the lifter of my head.[8] You give your holy angels charge over me, to keep me in all my ways.[9] I will say of you, O God, you are my refuge and my fortress, my God in whom I will trust.[10]

I rejoice in the encouragement your Word brings to me, Father.

References: *(1) 1 Peter 1:7; (2) Philippians 4:6-8; (3) Psalms 138:7; (4) Hebrews 10:35; (5) Philippians 1:6; (6) Psalms 31:24; (7) Psalms 27:11, 14; (8) Psalms 3:3; (9) Psalms 91:11; (10) Psalms 91:2.*

10. When You Feel Dissatisfied

Key Scripture: *"Trust in the Lord, and do good; so shalt thou dwell in the land, and verily thou shalt be fed" (Ps. 37:3).*

Key Thought: "The time of business does not with me differ from the time of prayer: and in the noise and clatter of my kitchen, while several persons are at the same time calling for different things, I possess God in as great tranquillity as if I were upon my knees" (Brother Lawrence).

Prayer: Heavenly Father, forgive me for feeling dissatisfied. I repent of my boredom and dissatisfaction as I once again realize that those who seek you shall not want any good thing.[1] O God, you are my God. Early I will seek you. My soul thirsts for you, and my flesh longs for you in a dry and thirsty land. I long to see your power and your glory. Your lovingkindness, dear Father, is better than life to me. Therefore, my lips will bless you and praise you. I will bless you as long as I live. I will lift up my hands in your name. As I do so, I know my soul will be satisfied as if with marrow and fatness, and my mouth will praise you with joyful lips.[2]

As I praise you, Lord, I am satisfied.[3] In your goodness, Father, I find complete satisfaction.[4] You enable me to eat in plenty and

to be satisfied. I praise your name, Lord.
Thank you for dealing so wondrously with
me. Because of your dealings in my life, I
know I shall never be ashamed.[5]

I bless you, O Lord. All that is within
me blesses you. I will not forget all your
benefits to me. You have forgiven me all my
iniquities, and healed my sicknesses. You
have redeemed my life from destruction,
and you have crowned me with your
lovingkindness and tender mercies. You are
my satisfaction, Father.[6]

*References: (1) Psalms 34:10; (2) Psalms 63:1-5;
(3) Proverbs 12:14; (4) Jeremiah 31:14; (5) Joel 2:26;
(6) Psalms 103:1-5.*

11. When You Need to Overcome Fear

Key Scripture: *"For God hath not given us the spirit of fear; but of power, and of love, and of a sound mind" (2 Tim. 1:7).*

Key Thought: Fear knocked at the door. Faith answered. No one was there.

Prayer: Dear Lord, I thank you and praise you for the fact that you are my light and my salvation. Of what, then, shall I be afraid? You are the strength of my life; of whom shall I be afraid?[1] I will not be afraid of sudden fear or any other kind of fear, because you, Lord, are my confidence and I know you will keep me safe at all times.[2]

You have given great peace to me and you have told me, "Don't let your heart be troubled and don't let your heart be afraid."[3] Thank you for the gift of peace you've given to me through your Son, Jesus Christ.

I am so very grateful, Father, that I have not received the spirit of bondage to fear. Instead, I have received the Spirit of adoption that causes me to cry, "Abba, Father." Thank you for adopting me into your family.[4] Father, I know you are my Helper; therefore, I will never fear what men can do to me.[5]

It's a wonderful realization to know that there is no fear in your love. In fact, I rejoice in the certainty that your perfect love casts out all fear from my life.[6]   Thank you for delivering me from the torments of fear. You have not given me a spirit of fear, for you have given me a spirit of power, of love, and of a sound mind.[7]   Fill me with your love now as I receive it by faith in your promise.[8]

References: *(1) Psalms 27:1; (2) Proverbs 3:25-26; (3) John 14:27; (4) Romans 8:15-16; (5) Hebrews 13:6; (6) 1 John 4:18; (7) 2 Timothy 1:7; (8) Mark 11:24.*

12. When You Need Guidance

Key Scripture: *"I will instruct thee and teach thee in the way which thou shalt go: I will guide thee with mine eye" (Ps. 32:8).*

Key Thought: "In general, he [God] guides and directs his people, by affording them, in answer to prayer, the light of his Holy Spirit, which enables them to understand and to love the Scriptures" (John Newton).

Prayer: Heavenly Father, I thank you for guiding my life and leading me at all times. Show me your way so that I might know your will.[1] I ask you to be my vision, my eyes, my all.[2] You are my lamp, O Lord.[3] You lead me beside the still waters, and you restore my soul.[4] Show me your ways, O Lord. Teach me your paths.[5] I thank you for the knowledge that you will guide me with judgment and you will teach me your ways.[6]

Your Word promises me, Lord, that you always order the steps of a good person, and you delight in the way of a person who is following you.[7] With all my heart, Father, I want to be the kind of person who brings joy and delight to your heart.

Send out your light and truth. Let them lead me.[8] You are my God forever and ever; you will be my guide even unto death.[9] Your Word is a lamp unto my feet, and a light unto my path.[10] Cause me to know the way in which I should walk.[11] Attend to my prayer, Father, as I incline my ear to your Word.[12]

You have given me the Holy spirit to guide me into all truth.[13] Thank you for His guiding presence in my life.[14]

References: *(1) Exodus 33:13; (2) Numbers 10:31; (3) 2 Samuel 22:29; (4) Psalms 23:2-3; (5) Psalms 25:4; (6) Psalms 25:9; (7) Psalms 37:23; (8) Psalms 43:3; (9) Psalms 48:14; (10) Psalms 119:105; (11) Psalms 143:8; (12) Proverbs 4:20; (13) John 16:13; (14) Romans 8:14.*

13. When You Feel Guilty

Key Scripture: *"If we confess our sins, he is faithful and just to forgive us our sins, and to cleanse us from all unrighteousness" (1 John 1:9).*

Key Thought: "John Bunyan and John Wesley were both plagued with the conviction that they could not be forgiven. When at last the realization that they were forgiven entered their tortured minds, they became new men with a gospel of liberation for tens of thousands of people" (Roy Trevivian).

Prayer: Dear Father, thank you for Jesus Christ, the righteous One, who is my personal Advocate when I sin. He is the atoning sacrifice for all my sins.[1] Hallelujah! What a Savior He is. I confess all my sins to you now, Father, and I receive your forgiveness as you cleanse me from all unrighteousness.[2] Through your grace, Lord, you have granted repentance to my heart and I have turned from my sins. Now I am determined to follow you and your ways at all times.

Thank you for your Word, Father. With your help, I will take heed to your Word, because I know this will keep me from sin. With my whole heart I will seek you; please don't let me wander from your commandments. I will diligently hide your Word in my heart so that I will not sin against you.[3]

How I praise you, Lord, for the realization that guilt no longer has any right to have dominion in my life. I will trust in your mercy forever.[4] You have set me free from guilt and condemnation because you love me. The sacrifice of Jesus for my sins has completely cleansed me, and now it is as if I had never sinned. Thank you for imputing your righteousness to me. Thank you for sending Jesus who knew no sin, but willingly became sin for me so that I could become righteous in you.[5]

Unto you, O Lord, I lift up my soul, for you are good, and you are always ready to forgive your children. You are plenteous in mercy unto all who call upon you.[6] Thank you for forgiving me of my iniquities and for remembering them no more. Lord, you have removed my sins from me as far as the east is from the west.[7] You have buried all my sins in the depths of the deepest sea. Help me to be like you by never remembering my sins any more.[8]

By faith, Lord, I declare that I am forgiven. I am restored.

References: *(1) 1 John 2:1-2; (2) 1 John 1:9; (3) Psalms 119:9-11; (4) Psalms 52:8; (5) 2 Corinthians 5:21; (6) Psalms 86:4-6; (7) Psalms 103:12; (8) Hebrews 8:12.*

14. When You Need Hope

Key Scripture: *"Why art thou cast down, O my soul? and why art thou disquieted within me? hope thou in God: for I shall yet praise him, who is the health of my countenance, and my God"* (Ps. 42:11).

Key Thought: Hope is the anchor of your soul. (See Heb. 6:19.)

Prayer: Let your mercy, O Lord, be upon me as I endeavor to experience the hope you promise to me.[1] You are my hiding place and my shield, and I find hope in your Word.[2]

Let my life be filled with your hope, joy, peace, and faith so that I will always continue to abound in hope through the power of your Holy Spirit.[3]

Thank you for equipping me with your protective armor, Father.[4] I put on the hope of salvation as my helmet.[5] Thank you for giving me everlasting consolation and good hope through your grace.[6]

Even now, as I pray, I experience your hope as being the sure and steadfast anchor of my soul.[7] From now on, I will hope continually, and I will praise you more and more.[8] Christ in me is the hope of glory.[9]

Father, thank you for exchanging my sense of hopelessness with your abiding hope.

References: *(1) Psalms 33:22; (2) Psalms 119:114; (3) Romans 15:13; (4) Ephesians 6:11; (5) Ephesians 6:17; (6) 2 Thessalonians 2:16; (7) Hebrews 6:19; (8) Psalms 71:14; (9) Colossians 1:27.*

15. When You Are Feeling Insecure

Key Scripture: *"Casting all your care upon him; for he careth for you" (1 Pet. 5:7).*

Key Thought: Each one of us matters to God, and because He does care, we can always feel secure.

Prayer: Heavenly Father, because my heart is fixed, trusting in you, I will not be afraid of any evil tidings.[1] Help me to trust you more and more because I know this is the key to security in my life.

Thank you for your promise that anyone who trusts in you will be like a tree planted by the waters, that spreads out its roots by the river.[2] Thank you for promising to direct my paths when I trust you with all my heart.[3] Father, this knowledge brings a feeling of great security to my soul.

Thank you for your promise that your great mercy will encompass me.[4] In place of any feeling of insecurity, I will continue in supplications and prayers night and day.[5] Grant that I would never place my trust in uncertain riches or any other thing, except you, my living God, who richly gives me all things to enjoy.[6]

I place all my trust in you, O Lord, because I realize that I am not sufficient of myself in anything. All my sufficiency and all my security are from you, Father.[7] You are my confidence, and I know that you will always keep me safe.[8]

Father, I take my stand upon your Word which is forever settled in heaven,[9] and in so doing, I feel completely secure. You are my security and my strong rock.[10]

Thank you, Lord God, that through faith in Christ I have boldness and access to you with confidence,[11] and this makes me secure.

References: *(1) Psalms 112:7; (2) Jeremiah 17:7-8; (3) Proverbs 3:5-6; (4) Psalms 32:10-11; (5) 1 Timothy 5:5; (6) 1 Timothy 6:17-18; (7) 2 Corinthians 3:5; (8) Proverbs 3:26; (9) Psalms 119:89; (10) Psalms 31:3; (11) Ephesians 3:12.*

16. When You Are Tempted to Feel Jealous

Key Scripture: *"A sound heart is the life of the flesh; but envy [jealousy] the rottenness of the bones" (Prov. 14:30).*

Key Thought: Jealousy is self-centered and does not trust God. (See Prov. 3:5-6.)

Prayer: Father, thank you for wanting to keep me free from all envy, jealousy, or covetousness in any form.[1] Help me to love others and to rejoice with them, and help me to remember that love is patient and kind at all times and that love never envies or feels jealous.[2] Forgive me for being jealous and envious of others, their possessions and their positions. I fully repent of all jealousy, envy, and covetousness in my life.[3]

Father, I choose to resist all jealousy by trusting you and knowing that you will always take good care of me.[4] As I take heed to your Word, Father, I learn how to beware of covetousness and jealousy. Your Word has taught me that a person's life does not consist in the abundance of things he possesses, but in living for you.[5] I thank you for the spiritual abundance you have blessed me with.

Father, I now realize that godliness with contentment is great gain for me.[6] I will always trust your provision, because I know you will always supply all of my needs according to your riches in glory, by Christ Jesus.[7]

Lord God, I thank you for the truth of your love that sets me free from all temptations of jealousy.[8]

Thank you for delivering me from jealousy, Father.

References: *(1) Titus 3:1-7; (2) 1 Corinthians 13:4; (3) Exodus 20:17; (4) Psalms 23:1; (5) Luke 12:15; (6) 1 Timothy 6:6-8; (7) Philippians 4:19; (8) John 8:32.*

17. When You Need Joy

Key Scripture: *"Yet believing, ye rejoice with joy unspeakable and full of glory" (1 Peter 1:8).*

Key Thought: Believing brings great joy.

Prayer: Lord, I want to be filled with your joy. Your joy is my strength, [1] and it is filled with glory.[2] Father, thank you for your kingdom, where I find righteousness, peace, and joy in your Holy Spirit.[3] Your wonderful salvation fills me with unspeakable joy.[4]

Let your Holy Spirit increase the fruit of joy in me.[5] Through your Word, I experience the deeper joy your Holy Spirit inspires within me. Thank you for this abiding joy which lifts me above life's circumstances.[6]

In your presence, Lord, there is fullness of joy.[7] Through your grace, I will walk in your presence each day. As I draw near to you now, I know you are drawing near to me.[8] Lord God, I love you, and I love being in your presence. I put my trust completely in you, and as I do so, I rejoice. You are my Defender, and I love your name. I will ever be joyful in you.[9]

References: (1) Nehemiah 8:10; (2) 1 Peter 1:8; (3) Romans 14:17; (4) 1 Peter 1:8-9; (5) Galatians 5:22; (6) 1 Thessalonians 1:6; (7) Psalms 16:11; (8) James 4:8; (9) Psalms 5:11.

18. When You Are Lonely

Key Scripture: *"Let your conversation be without covetousness; and be content with such things as ye have: for he hath said, I will never leave thee, nor forsake thee" (Heb. 13:5).*

Key Thought: God invades our loneliness with His presence.

Prayer: Lord, I thank you that you will never leave me alone nor forsake me. I know you will never let me down.[1] You do not leave me comfortless, but you have sent your Spirit, the Comforter, to be with me always.[2] I receive the loving presence of your Spirit now as I pray.[3] He is with me,[4] and He dwells within me.[5] Holy Spirit, I welcome your presence.

In the same way that Jesus turned to you, Father, when He was left alone in the Garden of Gethsemane, I will always seek you when I feel lonely.[6] When I come before your throne of grace I know that I will always find your mercy, comfort, and grace to minister to me in my times of need.[7] Thank you, Lord.

When your Son, my Lord and Savior, Jesus Christ, felt forsaken and lonely He did not despair because He knew you were always with Him.[8] I know you understand all my needs, and it is wonderful to walk with you. Let all loneliness that the enemy brings be gone from me, Lord. Tear down any thought-strongholds of loneliness as I pray.

My fellowship is with you, Father, and with your Son, Jesus Christ. Help me always to remember this truth so that my joy may be full.[9]

Thank you for delivering me from all loneliness, Father.

References: *(1) Hebrews 13:5; (2) John 14:16-18; (3) John 20:22; (4) John 14:16; (5) John 14:17; (6) Luke 22:41-42; (7) Hebrews 4:14-16; (8) Mark 14:50; (9) 1 John 1:3-4.*

19. When You Need to Know You're Loved

Key Scripture: *"There is no fear in love; but perfect love casteth out fear: because fear hath torment. He that feareth is not made perfect in love. We love him, because he first loved us"* (1 John 4:18-19).

Key Thought: God is love.

Prayer: Heavenly Father, you loved the world so much that you gave your only begotten Son, that whosoever would believe in Him should not perish, but have everlasting life.[1] Thank you for loving me so much. When I don't feel I'm loved, I need to remember always that you first loved me, and this fact of my faith enables me to love myself and others.[2] I receive your love, Father.

I truly love you, Father, and I thank you for loving me. I want to follow all your commandments because of your great love for me.[3] You have saved me and made me into a new creation; therefore, I can love others as you have loved me. By experiencing your love and sharing it with others people will know that I am a disciple of Jesus Christ.[4] Thank you, Father.

Your perfect love has cast out all fear from my life,[5] including the fear of not being loved. Thank you so much for your limitless love, Lord. It really is from everlasting to everlasting. Thank you for pouring your love into my heart through your Holy Spirit who you have given to me.[6] Through Him, I am able to comprehend with all saints the full extent of your love.[7]

Strengthen me by your Spirit in my innermost being, Father, and keep rooting and grounding me in your wonderful love. Above all else, I desire to know your love which surpasses knowledge. Fill me to the utmost with the fullness of your love and your presence.[8]

Thank you for loving me.

References: *(1) John 3:16; (2) 1 John 4:17-21; (3) John 14:15; (4) John 13:34-35; (5) 1 John 4:18; (6) Romans 5:5; (7) Ephesians 3:18-20; (8) Ephesians 3:17-20.*

20. When You Need Freedom From Lust

Key Scripture: *"But every man is tempted, when he is drawn away of his own lust, and enticed. Then when lust hath conceived, it bringeth forth sin: and sin, when it is finished, bringeth forth death" (James 1:14-15).*

Key Thought: Overcome lust with trust.

Prayer: Heavenly Father, thank you for your great faithfulness in my life. I rejoice in the certain knowledge that you will not permit me to be tempted above my ability to resist. When temptation comes you will make a way for me to escape, and this will enable me to bear it.[1] Help me always to learn from the truths and teaching of your Word, Father, which show me what happens when lust is fulfilled. Because of these realities, with your help, I will always flee from lust.[2]

Lord, I choose to flee from lust, because I know you will empower me to follow righteousness, faith, charity (love), and peace with all who call on you out of a pure heart.[3] I call upon you to enable me to abstain from all fleshly lusts which war against my soul.[4] I will treasure your truth, and I will hide your Word in my heart so that I might not sin against you.[5]

Help me, Lord, to be led of your Spirit so that I will not fulfill the temptations of lust.[6]

Through the power of your might,[7] I will stand fast in the liberty Christ has given to me, and I will no longer be entangled with the yoke of bondage.[8]

I rejoice, Father, that your truth has set me free.[9] Because of your mercies to me, I present my body as a living sacrifice, holy and acceptable to you. With your help, I will no longer be conformed to this world. Through the power of your Word, I am being transformed by the renewing of my mind.[10]

As I seek first your will, your kingdom, and your righteousness, I learn to put all lust behind me.[11] Forgive me, Lord, for the idolatry of lust in my life that has come as a result of my failure to put you and your righteousness first. Thank you for delivering me from the lusts of the eyes and the flesh.[12]

References: *(1) 1 Corinthians 10:6-13; (2) Romans 1:27-32; (3) 2 Timothy 2:22; (4) 1 Peter 2:11; (5) Psalms 119:11;(6) Galatians 5:16; (7) Ephesians 6:10; (8) Galatians 5:1; (9) John 8:32; (10) Romans 12:1-2; (11) Matthew 6:33; (12) 1 John 2:16.*

21. **When You Need Patience**

Key Scripture: *"That ye be not slothful, but followers of them who through faith and patience inherit the promises" (Heb. 6:12).*

Key Thought: The path to God's promises is paved with patience.

Prayer: Heavenly Father, thank you for giving me patience as a fruit of your Holy Spirit.[1] Continue to work your patience in me so that I may accomplish your will and inherit your promises.[2]

Father, I will hear your Word and obey it, so that I will be able to bring forth fruit with patience.[3] Likewise, I will obey your command to possess my soul through patience.[4] Therefore, I will let patience have its perfect work in my life so that I will become perfect and entire, wanting nothing.[5]

Through your grace, Father, I will run with patience the race you have set before me. I will keep my eyes on Jesus, who is the Author and Finisher of my faith.[6] I will wait on you, Lord, and I know that as I wait, you will strengthen my heart to walk in patience.[7] I believe all the promises of your Word, and I know that they will never fail. Thank you for each and every promise you've give to me, for I know that all of your promises in Christ Jesus are yes and amen.[8]

As I wait upon you, Lord, you are renewing my strength. I am mounting up with wings like an eagle. When I run, I will not be weary, and when I walk, I will not faint.[9] Thank you for supplying my need for patience. I will walk in the patience you've imparted to me each day of my life.

References: (1) Galatians 5:22; (2) Hebrews 10:36; (3) Luke 8:15; (4) Luke 21:19; (5) James 1:4; (6) Hebrews 12:1-2; (7) Psalms 27:14; (8) 2 Corinthians 1:20; (9) Isaiah 40:31.

22. When You Need Peace of Mind

Key Scripture: *"Peace I leave with you, my peace I give unto you: not as the world giveth, give I unto you. Let not your heart be troubled, neither let it be afraid" (John 14:27).*

Key Thought: The believer has peace that the world can't give, and the world can't take it away.

Prayer: Heavenly Father, thank you for your peace which surpasses all understanding and keeps my heart and mind through Christ Jesus.[1] You always keep me in perfect peace when I keep my mind stayed on you in an attitude of complete trust in you.[2] Peace of mind is very precious to me, Lord, so I ask you to help me to trust you always.

Father, help me to follow the guidance your peace in my heart brings to me.[3] Thank you for ordaining peace for me,[4] and giving me peace like a river,[5] because I love your Word.[6]

I will always have peace with you, Father, through my Lord and Savior Jesus Christ.[7] I delight myself in the abundant peace you give to me.[8] Thank you for the fruit of peace you give to me through your Holy Spirit.[9] I receive His provision of peace as I pray.[10]

God of all hope, I praise you for filling me with your joy and peace that come through believing your Word. I now abound in hope and peace through the power of your Holy Spirit.[11] I receive your promise of peace of mind, Lord. Thank you for your blessing of peace in my life.

References: *(1) Philippians 4:7 (2) Isaiah 26:3-4; (3) Colossians 3:15; (4) Isaiah 26:12; (5) Isaiah 48:18; (6) Psalms 119:165; (7) Romans 5:1; (8) Psalms 37:11; (9) Galatians 5:22; (10) John 14:27; (11) Romans 15:13.*

23. When You've Experienced Rejection

Key Scripture: *"For we have not an high priest which cannot be touched with the feeling of our infirmities; but was in all points tempted like as we are, yet without sin. Let us therefore come boldly unto the throne of grace, that we may obtain mercy, and find grace to help in time of need"* (Heb. 4:15-16).

Key Thought: Jesus heals all our wounds.

Prayer: Heavenly Father, the rejection I've experienced is very painful, and I need your healing touch. Through Jesus Christ, you heal the broken-hearted,[1] and you bind up all my wounds.[2]

Thank you for Jesus Christ who is my High Priest, and was despised and rejected of men. He understands my rejection, and He bears my grief and carries my sorrow.[3]

Father, the rejection I have experienced from: _____has caused me great pain, and I know this touches your heart. Therefore, through faith and an act of my will, in obedience to your Word, I choose to forgive _____ _____[4] for the pain his/her words and actions have brought to me. I receive your healing, Lord,[5] and I pray for _____ _____, asking you to bless him/her with a knowledge of your will in all things.[6]

O Lord, teach me your ways, and lead me in a plain path.[7] I will seek your face. Lord God, because you are my help, and you are my salvation, when others forsake or reject me, I know you will lift me up.[8] You are my refuge, and underneath me are your everlasting arms.[9]

Thank you for healing me of the pain of rejection, Lord.

References: *(1) Luke 4:18; (2) Psalms 147:3; (3) Isaiah 53:3-4; (4) Ephesians 4:32; (5) Mark 11:24; (6) Colossians 1:9; (7) Psalms 27:11; (8) Psalms 27:9-10; (9) Deuteronomy 33:27.*

24. When You Don't Feel
Good About Yourself

Key Scripture: *"I will praise thee; for I am fearfully and wonderfully made: marvellous are thy works; and that my soul knoweth right well"* *(Ps. 139:14).*

Key Thought: "But with you, Lord, there are no walls. You, who made me, know my deepest emotions, my most secret thoughts. You know the good of me and the bad of me, you already understand . . . . From your perfect understanding I receive understanding for my own life's needs" (Marjorie Holmes).

Prayer: Heavenly Father, I believe your Word which tells me that you love me,[1] and that nothing can separate me from your love,[2] except my own refusal to believe it and to receive it.

You loved me even before I was born, and you fashioned me according to your grand plan and purpose. I am one of your marvelous works, Father, and I praise you because I am fearfully and wonderfully made.[3]

Thank you for making me a new creation in Christ. I rejoice in the certain knowledge that you have made all things new in my life,[4] including the way I see myself. I have been made complete in Christ.[5]

Thank you for loving me and helping me to love you with all my heart, to love myself as you love me,[6] and for helping me to like myself as well. From this time forward, I will walk in love toward you, others, and myself, because I know Christ loved me and gave himself for me.[7]

I trust you, Father, to continue your workmanship in my life, for I know that you are working within me, both to will and to do your good pleasure and desires.[8]

References: *(1) John 3:16; (2) Romans 8:38-39; (3) Psalms 139:13-16; (4) 2 Corinthians 5:17; (5) Colossians 2:10; (6) Matthew 19:19; (7) Ephesians 5:2; (8) Philippians 2:13.*

25. When Troubles Come Your Way

Key Scripture: *"Let not your heart be troubled: ye believe in God, believe also in me" (John 14:1).*

Key Thought: "The true way to soften one's troubles is to solace those of others" (Mme. de Maintenon).

Prayer: Though I walk in the midst of trouble, I know you will revive me, Lord. I believe you will stretch forth your right hand which will save me from all my troubles.[1] Thank you, Father. You are so good to me. Thank you for being my stronghold in the day of trouble. I place my complete trust in you.[2]

Father, I believe your promise that all things do work together for good to those who love you. Thank you for calling me according to your purposes.[3] I bless you, Father, for I know you are the Father of my Lord and Savior, Jesus Christ. You are the Father of mercies and the God of all comfort. You are comforting me in this time of trouble and tribulation. Help me to comfort others in the same way you are comforting me.[4]

My help comes from you, Lord. You are my all-powerful Father, who made heaven and earth.[5] Thank you, Lord. I am glad as I rejoice in your mercy. I know you are aware of the troubles I face,[6] and because you are, I am able to come boldly before your throne of grace, realizing that I will receive your mercy and your grace to help me in my time of need.[7]

I cast all my cares upon you because I know you care for me.[8] I know that no weapon that is formed against me will prosper, for this is my heritage as your servant, O Lord.[9] Thank you, Father.

References: *(1) Psalms 138:7; (2) Nahum 1:7; (3) Romans 8:28; (4) 2 Corinthians 1:3-4; (5) Psalms 121:1-2; (6) Psalms 31:7; (7) Hebrews 4:15-16; (8) 1 Peter 5:7; (9) Isaiah 54:17.*

26. When You Are Worried

Key Scripture: *"Be careful for nothing; but in every thing by prayer and supplication with thanksgiving let your requests be made known unto God. And the peace of God, which passeth all understanding, shall keep your hearts and minds through Christ Jesus" (Phil. 4:6-7).*

Key Thought: "If you take your problem to God, leave it with God. You have no right to brood over it any longer" (Martyn Lloyd-Jones).

Prayer: Heavenly Father, thank you for your promise of freedom from worry,[1] and fear.[2] Your care for me leads me to know that I can cast all my worries upon you.[3] Forgive me for worrying; I know I don't have to bear my burdens alone. Thank you for inviting me to come unto you, and for your wonderful promise of rest.[4] I receive your peaceful rest as I lay down my burdens and worries.

Your Word assures me that nothing shall be able to separate me from your love, which is in Christ Jesus my Lord.[5] You have promised to supply all my needs,[6] and I know that you know all my needs even before I tell them to you.[7]

Father, your perfect love casts out all my fears and worries.[8] In fact, you have commanded me not to worry, because it is your good pleasure to give me your kingdom.[9]

The great and precious promises of your Word thrill me, Father.[10]

Instead of wasting my time with worry, I will give myself to prayer, and let my requests be known unto you, with thanksgiving. Lord, how truly thankful I am that your peace will keep my heart and mind through Christ Jesus.[11] I praise you for taking all my worries as I cast them upon you.[12]

References: *(1) Philippians 4:6-7; (2) 1 John 4:18; (3) 1 Peter 5:7; (4) Matthew 11:28; (5) Romans 8:38-39; (6) Philippians 4:19; (7) Matthew 6:8; (8) 1 John 4:18; (9) Luke 12:32; (10) 2 Peter 1:4; (11) Philippians 4:6-7; (12) 1 Peter 5:7.*

PHYSICAL NEEDS

1. When You Need Better Health

Key Scripture: *"Bless the Lord, O my soul, And forget not all His benefits: Who forgives all your iniquities, Who heals all your diseases" (Ps. 103:2-3, NKJV).*

Key Thought: God wants you to be healthy.

Prayer: Heavenly Father, thank you for your promise that you will always hasten your Word to the one in need.[1] I thank you for your Word which is alive and powerful, and I know it is sharper than any two-edged sword.[2] I believe that your Word teaches me that healing and health are your children's bread,[3] and that you are the Lord who heals me.[4]

Thank you for Jesus who provides health for me. I praise you that He took all my infirmities and bore all my sicknesses.[5] I believe your Word, Father, because it assures me that whatever things I desire, when I pray, to believe I will receive them from you, Father, and I will have them.[6] I ask you for improved health and healing in every area of my life, and I receive your promise that healing and health are mine.

Thank you for restoring my health and vitality to me. My faith does not rest in the wisdom of people, Lord, but in the great power of your Word and Spirit.[7] I know that all healing and health come from you, Father,[8] and I know you love me and want me to be healthy at all times. As I wait upon you, my strength is being renewed, and I am mounting up with wings like an eagle.[9] You are making my heart merry, and this does me good like a medicine.[10] Through your Spirit, my body is being quickened,[11] and I am experiencing the resurrection-power of Jesus Christ, my Lord.[12]

Thank you for the health you are imparting to me, Father.

References: *(1) Jeremiah 1:2; (2) Hebrews 4:12; (3) Mark 7:27; (4) Exodus 15:26; (5) Matthew 8:17; (6) Mark 11:24; (7) 1 Corinthians 2:5; (8) Psalms 103:3; (9) Isaiah 40:31; (10) Proverbs 17:22; (11) Romans 8:11; (12) Philippians 3:10.*

2. God's All-Sufficient Grace

Key Scripture: *"And He said to me, 'My grace is sufficient for you, for My strength is made perfect in weakness'" (2 Cor. 12:9, NKJV).*

Key Thought: God's grace is all-sufficient.

Prayer: O Lord, my gracious God,[1] thank you for your grace which is greater than all my sin or sickness.[2] I rejoice in the marvelous grace you have bestowed upon my life.[3] All of your promises are for me.[4] I truly abound in your grace,[5] O Lord, which is always sufficient for me.[6] Your grace, O Lord, is enough in any situation. When I feel weak, I will be glad and glorify your name, so that the power of Christ, my Savior, will rest upon me. Thank you for your Son, my Lord and Savior, Jesus Christ, who is gracious like you are, Father.[7]

Thank you for His willingness to impart His grace to me. Even though He was rich, for my sake, He became poor so that, through His poverty, I might be made rich and abundantly supplied.[8] Thank you, Father. This is true grace in my life, and I fully and thankfully receive it as a treasure I cannot earn. It is a gift of your great love for me.[9]

Yes, I know your grace is sufficient for me, Father.[10] By your grace, through faith, I was saved.[11] Your unmerited favor (grace) in my life has provided me with the wonderful gift of salvation.[12] Like Noah of old, I have found grace in your sight, Father.[13] Thank you so much.

My Savior is your Son, Jesus Christ, who is also your incarnate Word, and He is full of grace and truth.[14] Thank you for allowing me to receive of His fullness — grace for grace.[15] How thankful I am, Lord, that I have been justified freely by the grace of Jesus Christ.[16] Because of your loving mercy and grace, Father, my peace is constantly being multiplied.[17] Thank you, God, for the power of your grace which always keeps me.[18]

I rejoice in your grace, Father.

References: *(1) Exodus 34:6; (2) Ephesians 2:5; (3) 2 Corinthians 8:1; (4) 2 Corinthians 7:1; (5) 2 Corinthians 8:7; (6) 2 Corinthians 12:9; (7) 2 Thessalonians 3:18; (8) 2 Corinthians 8:9; (9) Romans 6:23; (10) 2 Corinthians 12:9; (11) Ephesians 2:8; (12) Ephesians 2:8; (13) Genesis 6:8; (14) John 1:14; (15) Romans 3:24; (16) Romans 5:17; (17) 2 Peter 1:2; (18) 1 Peter 1:5.*

3. When You Need Healing

Key Scripture: *"Bless the Lord, O my soul: and all that is within me, bless his holy name. Bless the Lord, O my soul, and forget not all his benefits: Who forgiveth all thine iniquities; who healeth all thy diseases" (Ps. 103:1-3).*

Key Thought: All healing comes from God.

Prayer: Heavenly Father, thank you for your Word which tells me that healing is your children's bread.[1] The Scriptures point out that you are the Lord who heals me.[2] Your Word tells me that I experience healing through the stripes of Jesus Christ.[3]

I praise you, God, that Jesus Christ has taken my infirmities and carried my diseases.[4] I praise you that He is the same yesterday, today, and forever.[5] He was wounded for my transgressions, He was bruised for my iniquities. The chastisement of my peace was upon Him, and by His stripes I am healed.[6]

Heal me, O Lord, and I shall be healed. Save me, and I shall be saved, for your are my praise.[7]

I receive the healing you have for me.[8] Your Word tells me that you want me to walk in health, and as I hearken unto your voice and do what is right in your sight, you will keep disease from me.[9] Thank you, Father.

Bless the Lord, O my soul, and forget not all His benefits.[10] You forgive me of all my iniquities, and you heal all of my diseases.[11] Thank you and bless you, Father, for redeeming my life from destruction and crowning me with your lovingkindness and your tender mercies.[12]

Praise your name, O Lord. I love you and thank you for healing me and keeping me in good health.

References: *(1) Mark 7:27; (2) Exodus 15:26; (3) Isaiah 53:5; (4) Matthew 8:17; (5) Hebrews 13:8; (6) Isaiah 53:5; (7) Jeremiah 17:14; (8) Mark 11:24; (9) Exodus 15:26; (10) Psalms 103:1; (11) Psalms 103:3; (12) Psalms 103:4.*

4. Healing for a Loved One

Key Scripture: *"And the prayer of faith shall save the sick, and the Lord shall raise him up; and if he have committed sins, they shall be forgiven him" (James 5:15).*

Key Thought: Jesus is the Great Physician.

Prayer: Lord God, in your Word you instruct us to pray for one another's healing. I thank you that the effectual, fervent prayers of those who have been made righteous through faith in Jesus Christ are powerful and effective.[1] Your Word declares, O God, that with the stripes of Jesus we are healed.[2]

In behalf of _____, I express faith to you that he/she will be healed, and you will raise him/her up.[3]   I now ask for his/her complete healing in the name of Jesus Christ.[4]

Help _____ to remember your works, O Lord, and to meditate upon your doings.[5]   Build faith in his/her heart to realize that you are able to do all things exceedingly abundantly above all that we can ask or think, through your power that works within us.[6]

Thank you for Jesus who took all our infirmities and carried our diseases away.[7] Remind _____ of Jesus' example and the truth of this great promise.

Thank you, Father, for the fact that Jesus is the same yesterday, today, and forever.[8]

You are the God who does wonders, and you have declared your strength among the people.[9] I hope in you, Lord, and I will ever praise you.[10] Thank you for bringing health to _____, and for healing him/her. Glory be to your name forever and ever.

References: (1) James 5:16; (2) Isaiah 53:5; (3) James 5:15; (4) John 15:16; (5) Psalms 77:11-12; (6) Ephesians 3:20; (7) Matthew 8:17; (8) Hebrews 13:8; (9) Psalms 77:14; (10) Psalms 42:11.

5. When You Need Mental Healing

Key Scripture: *"And the peace of God, which passeth all understanding, shall keep your hearts and minds through Christ Jesus" (Phil. 4:7).*

Key Thought: God heals the whole person.

Prayer: Heavenly Father, through faith in your name and your Word, I will be strong. As I pray, Lord, I receive the perfect soundness of mind and body you have for me.[1] In Christ Jesus, you have provided a way for me to be completely free from all depression, anxiety, guilt, worry, and every mental disorder.[2] Indeed, your truth makes me free. [3]

You have not given me a spirit of fear, but of power, and of love, and of a sound and healthy mind.[4] Thank you for your promise of healing which I receive by faith.[5] Father, I believe you are healing my mind, and binding up my wounds.[6]

Father, I bless you, for you are the Father of my Lord Jesus Christ, the Father of mercies, and the God of all comfort. I receive your comfort and your truth.[7]

I will not fear nor be dismayed, because I know that you are with me. You are my God, and even as I pray, you are strengthening me. Thank you for helping me, and upholding me with the right hand of your righteousness.[8]

You are a very present help to me.[9] I cast all of my burdens upon you, Father, and I know you will sustain me.[10]

Through faith in your Word, I will joyously proclaim, "I have the mind of Christ."[11]

References: *(1) Acts 3:16; (2) Isaiah 53:4-5; (3) John 8:32; (4) 2 Timothy 1:7; (5) James 5:15; (6) Psalms 147:3; (7) 2 Corinthians 1:3; (8) Isaiah 41:10; (9) Psalms 46:1; (10) Psalms 55:22; (11) 1 Corinthians 2:16.*

6. When You Need a Good Night's Sleep

Key Scripture: *"When thou liest down, thou shalt not be afraid: yea, thou shalt lie down, and thy sleep shall be sweet" (Prov. 3:24).*

Key Thought: Sleep is a blessing of God.

Prayer: Heavenly Father, I thank you that you give me deep, peaceful sleep.[1] I believe and I receive your promises of sleep and rest.

Help me to remember, Lord, when I am troubled or anxious, when circumstances seem to close in on me, or I have more to do than I seem to be able to cope with, that it is vain to rise up early, to sit up late, to eat the bread of sorrows, for you promise to give sleep to your beloved.[2] I thank you for the realization that I do not ever have to worry or to fret. When I rise up early, let it be for the joy of meeting you, Father.[3] If I sit up late, let it be because your Spirit has called me into communion[4] — but may it never be for worry or for self-indulgence.

Thank you for the peace Jesus gives to me.[5] When troubles or cares press in to hinder my sleep, I will cast my cares upon you, for I know you care for me,[6] and this knowledge gives me a peace that surpasses all understanding.[7]

With your help, Father, I will let your peace become my life-style, so that when I lie down I will not be afraid, and my sleep will be sweet because I trust in you.[8]

You have satisfied my weary soul, and you have replenished me. Thank you for removing all weariness from me. Thank you, also, for enabling me to lie down in peace and sleep. You alone, Lord, make me to dwell in safety,[10] and the sleep you give to me is sweet.[11]

References: *(1) 1 Samuel 26:12; (2) Psalms 127:2; (3) Proverbs 8:17; (4) Psalms 4:3-4; (5) John 14:27; (6) 1 Peter 5:7; (7) Philippians 4:7; (8) Proverbs 3:22-24; (9) Jeremiah 31:25; (10) Psalms 4:8; (11) Jeremiah 31:26.*

7. When You Feel Weak

Key Scripture: *"My grace is sufficient for you, for My strength is made perfect in weakness . . . . For when I am weak, then I am strong" (2 Cor. 12:9-10, NKJV).*

Key Thought: Your weakness is God's opportunity to be strong in your behalf.

Prayer: Father, thank you for showing me that without Christ I can do nothing,[1] but through Him I can do all things because He strengthens me.[2] Lord, continue to gird me with strength when I am weak, and make my way perfect.[3] Thank you for making my feet like the feet of a hind as you set me upon high places.[4] Thank you for teaching my hands to war so that I can break a steel bow in my arms.[5]

Father, you are the source of my strength.[6] You are my refuge and my strength, and you are a very present help to me in times of trouble.[7] Thank you, Father. When my strength fails and I feel weak, I know you will not forsake me.[8] You, Lord, are the source of all strength in my life. You are my refuge in the storm, and my shadow from the heat.[9] When I feel weak, I will say that I am strong because I know you are with me.[10]

I wait upon you, O Lord, and as I do so, you are strengthening my heart.[11] I will be of good courage because all my hope is in you.[12] Thank you for strengthening me according to the promises of your Word.[13] I will not fear because you are with me. I will not be dismayed because you are my God. You are strengthening me during this time of weakness. You are helping me during my time of need. You are upholding me with the right hand of your righteousness.[14]

Thank you for being my strength, dear Father.

References: (1) John 15:5; (2) Philippians 4:13; (3) Psalms 18:32; (4) Psalms 18:33; (5) Psalms 18:34; (6) Psalms 43:2; (7) Psalms 46:1; (8) Psalms 71:9; (9) Isaiah 25:4; (10) Joel 3:10; (11) Psalms 27:14; (12) Psalms 31:24; (13) Psalms 119:28; (14) Isaiah 41:10.

FINANCIAL NEEDS

1. Abundance

Key Scripture: *"The thief cometh not, but for to steal, and to kill, and to destroy: I am come that they might have life, and that they might have it more abundantly" (John 10:10).*

Key Thought: God wants you to abound with blessings!

Prayer: Heavenly Father, you are my Shepherd.[1] Because of your protective care[2] and supply[3] in my life I know I will never have to want for anything.[4] You always supply all my needs.[5] You are immeasurably great,[6] and you are greatly to be praised.[7]

Thank you for all your unsearchable riches that you've given for me to enjoy.[8] I claim your promises, and receive all the abundant treasures you've given to me.[9] Thank you for meeting all my needs.[10] I have abundant life from your hands, and you've given me abundance in all things.[11] Thank you, Father.

My God, you are the Father of lights with whom there is no variation or shadow of turning.[12] I recognize you to be the Giver of every good and perfect gift.[13] I rejoice in the realization that you want me to enjoy your abundant life in the here-and-now. Thank you for sending Jesus to give me abundant life.[14]

I receive your abundance, Father, as I claim your promises for my own. Thank you for giving me fullness,[15] wholeness,[16] and abundance in every area of my life. Living with your Son, Jesus, is an abundant life that gives me unspeakable joy and inexpressible glory.[17] Knowing you, Lord, fills my heart with gratitude. I am thankful in the certainty that you, my loving Father,[18] want me to prosper and enjoy good health at all times.[19]

Thank you for blessing me abundantly.

References: *(1) John 10:11; (2) 1 Peter 5:7; (3) 2 Corinthians 8:9; (4) Deuteronomy 8:9; (5) Philippians 4:19; (6) 1 Chronicles 29:11; (7) Psalms 48:1; (8) Proverbs 8:18; (9) Matthew 6:20; (10) Job 36:11; (11) Isaiah 48:15; (12) James 1:17; (13) James 1;17; (14) John 10:10; (15) John 1:16; (16) Mark 5:34; (17) 1 Peter 1:8; (18) 2 Corinthians 1:2; (19) 3 John 2.*

2. Your Daily Needs

Key Scripture: *"But my God shall supply all your need according to his riches in glory by Christ Jesus" (Phil. 4:19).*

Key Thought: God know our needs before we ask Him. (See Matt. 6:8.)

Prayer: Lord God, you are my faithful Father. You keep all your promises and your covenant with me.[1] Thank you for your daily provision in my life, and for always providing my daily bread.[2]. I rejoice in the knowledge that you always supply all of my needs according to your riches in glory by Christ Jesus, my Lord.[3]

It's a great comfort to me to know that you know all of my needs even before I express them to you.[4] I delight in the truth that you wish above all things that I would prosper and be in health, and that my soul would prosper too.[5] Father, thank you for your Word which declares that if I will trust in you and do good, I will dwell securely in the land and be fed. I delight myself in you, Lord, and I thrill to realize that you are giving me the desires of my heart. Hallelujah! I commit my way to you, and I trust in you;[6] therefore, I know that you will bring everything I need to fruition in my life.

I bless you, Father, for you have blessed me with every spiritual blessing in Christ Jesus, my Lord.[7] You have made me a new creation in Christ,[8] born again of your incorruptible Word.[9] Your mercy, O Lord, is in the heavens; and your faithfulness reaches unto the clouds.[10] I praise you for the joyful certainty that you are able to do exceedingly abundantly above all that I ask or think, according to your power which is at work in my life.[11] I delight in you, Lord, and I know that you will give me the desires of my heart.[12]

Thank you, Father.

References: *(1) Deuteronomy 7:9; (2) Luke 11:3; (3) Philippians 4:19; (4) Matthew 6:8; (5) 3 John 2; (6) Psalms 37:3-5; (7) Ephesians 1:3; (8) 2 Corinthians 5:17; (9) 1 Peter 1:23; (10) Psalms 36:5; (11) Ephesians 3:20; (12) Psalms 37:4.*

3. Faith for Your Finances

Key Scripture: *"Without faith it is impossible to please him: for he that cometh to God must believe that he is, and that he is a rewarder of them that diligently seek him" (Heb. 11:6).*

Key Thought: Faith comes through hearing God's Word. (See Rom. 10:17.)

Prayer: Your Word, O Lord, unlocks the doors of faith for me to enter. When I pray for wisdom regarding my finances or any other thing, help me to remember to ask you in faith, without any wavering. I ask you for the faith I need for my finances now, Lord, and I believe you will lead me, guide me, and bless me.[1]

Help me to remember that when my faith wavers, I cannot receive from you. But I am one who can receive, because I am a believer, not a doubter. Whenever doubt tries to come my way, I will cast it away because I realize it is an enemy that exalts itself against you, Father.[2]   Through your grace, I will continue to believe in you and the precious promises of your Word.

Help me always to remember that the just will live by their faith in you, Father.[3] May I always have faith to move mountains, to realize that nothing is impossible to one who walks in faith.[4] I look to the example of young

Stephen, Lord, as a man who was full of faith and power, a man who did great wonders in your name, and I want to be like him.[5]

Thank you for showing me that whatsoever is not of faith is sin.[6] It is my heart-felt desire, Lord, to continue in your faith, grounded and settled, and not to be moved away from the hope of your gospel.[7] Keep me steadfast in my faith, Lord, as I walk in Christ and continue to be rooted and built up in Him. Establish me in your faith; let me always abound in thanksgiving for your great gifts to me. You have revealed yourself to me in so many ways — through your Word, your Spirit, and all the changes you've wrought in my life. I believe in you with all my heart, and I will walk in faith each day, for I realize that faith is the victory that overcomes the world.[8]

Father, my faith in you and the promises of your Word assures me that you will bless me with abundance and prosperity.[9] Thank you, Lord.

References: *(1) James 1:5-8; (2) 2 Corinthians 10:5; (3) Habakkuk 2:4; (4) Matthew 17:20; (5) Acts 6:8; (6) Romans 14:22-23; (7) Colossians 1:23; (8) 1 John 5:4; (9) Psalms 1.*

4. Freedom From Financial Pressures

Key Scripture: *"But seek ye first the kingdom of God, and his righteousness; and all these things shall be added unto you" (Matt. 6:33).*

Key Thought: God will help you in every situation.

Prayer: O God, you are well able to take care of all my financial pressures. You know exactly what needs to be done and what steps need to be taken. I trust you to direct me in this situation.[1] Help me to always remember, Lord, that in your economy, resources are meant to flow freely from the place of excess to the place of need.[2] This truth gives me great hope.

In spite of financial pressures, I thank you that you do have a financial plan for my life, Lord, and I know you are able to make all grace abound toward me.[3] Thank you, Father.

Help me, Lord, to manage my financial resources better so that I will be free to serve you more fully and to give to the important causes of your kingdom. As I respond in obedience to your Word, I ask you to command your blessing upon my finances and upon all that I do.[4]

Deliver me, O my God,[5] for your are my hope.[6] When pressures threaten to overwhelm me, I will hope continually, and I will praise you more and more.[7] I will cast all my cares and worries on you, Father, because I know that you will always take care of me.[8]

The hope you've given to me leads me to trust you in every area of my life. I, therefore, place my unswerving trust in you, Father,[9] because you are my strength in the midst of trouble.[10]

As you walk with me in this situation, I will keep my mind focused upon you, I will trust in you, and I know you will keep me in your perfect peace.[11]

References: (1) Proverbs 3:5-6; (2) 2 Corinthians 8:14; (3) 2 Corinthians 9:7-8; (4) Deuteronomy 28:8; (5) Psalms 71:4; (6) Psalms 71:5; (7) Psalms 71:14; (8) 1 Peter 5:7; (9) Psalms 31:1; (10) Psalms 37:39; (11) Isaiah 26:3.

5. The Need to Give

Key Scripture: *"Bring ye all the tithes into the storehouse, that there may be meat in mine house, and prove me now herewith, saith the Lord of hosts, if I will not open you the windows of heaven, and pour you out a blessing, that there shall not be room enough to receive it" (Mal. 3:8-10).*

Key Thought: God always blesses His financial plan.

Prayer: Heavenly Father, everything I am and have belongs to you. Therefore, I will always remember to return the first-fruits to you.[1] I will tithe my income, Lord, as an act of obedience to you, and an avenue of blessing.[2] In response to your financial plan, I will give both tithes and offerings unto you, and I purpose in my heart to give to you regularly, Lord, and to always give cheerfully, without ever resenting what I give.[3]

In obedience to your Word, I will lay up treasures in heaven, where moth and rust cannot corrupt them, and where no thief can steal them.[4]

I will be sensitive to your direction in all my giving, Lord. I know that my giving is an act of worship to you, and what a privilege it is for me to be able to give. As I give, I will rejoice, and I will remember all the blessings you have given to me.[5]

Let your blessing be upon my giving, Lord. I will always remember that it is you who gives me the power to obtain wealth in order that your covenant may be fulfilled.[6] Let me use wisely all that you have given to me so as to bless the work of your kingdom and to help those in need.[7]

Thank you for showing me that love always gives. In fact, you loved the world so much that you gave your only Son.[8] Because of this truth, I give cheerfully and generously, and I know I will receive good measure, pressed down, shaken together, and running over. Help me to remember that the same measure I give out will be measured back to me.[9]

Trusting fully in your promises, Lord, I can freely give and freely receive.[10] I know that you will supply all of my needs according to your riches in glory by Christ Jesus. Your financial plan of giving and receiving is truly amazing, Father, and I thank you so much for your love and your provision.[11]

References: *(1) Deuteronomy 26; (2) Malachi 3:8-10; (3) 2 Corinthians 9:7; (4) Matthew 6:19-20; (5) Deuteronomy 28:2-8; (6) Deuteronomy 8:18; (7) James 4:3; (8) John 3:16; (9) Luke 6:38; (10) Matthew 10:8; (11) Philippians 4:19.*

6. Prosperity

Key Scripture: *"Beloved, I wish above all things that thou mayest prosper and be in health, even as thy soul prospereth" (3 John 2).*

Key Thought: God wants to prosper you.

Prayer: Heavenly Father, thank you for wanting me to prosper.[1] I seek you with all my heart, and in so doing I know you will not withhold any good thing from me, because I love you.[2] I will seek first your kingdom and your righteousness, and I know everything I need will be provided for me.[3] Loving Father, thank you for your promise to supply all my needs according to your riches in glory by Christ Jesus.[4]

I know you know all my needs.[5] Thank you and praise you, Father, for your great faithfulness to me.[6] You desire for me to prosper in all things, including my health, even as my soul prospers.[7] Thank you, Father.

Thank you for bringing me into a good land where there are brooks of water, flowing fountains, and abounding springs. It is a land of wheat, barley, vines, fig trees, pomegranates, olive oil, and honey. It is a place of abundance where there is plentiful bread to eat, and where there is no lack of any good thing. The stones in this land are iron, and there is brass in its hills. Jehovah-jireh, my Provider, thank you for prospering me in this rich land you have provided for me. Here, I can eat to the full and still have plenty left over. For all these reasons I praise and bless your name, O Lord. I will never forget you. I will keep all your commandments, your judgments, and your statutes. Thank you for the promise that you will multiply my herds and flocks. You will increase my silver and gold. All that I own will be multiplied. My heart is lifted up by your graciousness to me. You brought me out of captivity in the land of Egypt and brought me into the land of promise. It is you, the Lord, my God, who gives me the power to be wealthy, because this is a part of your eternal covenant with me, and with all who call upon you.[8]

Father, I will bless you at all times. Your praise shall continually be in my mouth.[9] My soul will make its boast in you.[10] I will magnify you and exalt your name.[11] Your lovingkindness is better than life to me.[12] In Jesus' name I pray,[13] Amen.

References: *(1) Psalms 23:1; (2) Psalms 34:10; (3) Matthew 6:33; (4) Philippians 4:19; (5) Matthew 6:8; (6) Lamentations 3:23; (7) 3 John 2; (8) Deuteronomy 8:7-14; (9) Psalms 34:1; (10) Psalms 34:2; (11) Psalms 34:3; (12) Psalms 63:3; (13) John 16:24.*

7. God's Provision

Key Scripture: *"And my God shall supply all your need according to His riches in glory by Christ Jesus"* (Phil. 4:19, NKJV).

Key Thought: God will provide.

Prayer: Great is your faithfulness, O God, my Father. Morning by morning new mercies I see.[1] I know that your hands will supply all that I need.[2] Thank you, Lord, for your loving care and supply in my life.[3] I claim the promises of your Word today.[4] I believe your Word,[5] and I look forward to all you are going to do in my life.[6]

You are Jehovah-jireh, my Provider.[7] You know exactly what I need, when I need it, and how my needs will best be met.[8] Thank you for the delight you experience as you give me the desires of my heart. I love you, and you love me.[9]

Thank you, Father, for your great mercies which are new in my life each morning.[10] Your grace and loving favor are upon me and within me.[11] Indeed, your lovingkindness is better than life to me.[12] Thank you for always providing me with my daily bread,[13] and so much more. I rejoice in you and in the knowledge that you are the God of more than enough.[14]

Thank you, Father, for caring about me and my loved ones.[15] I know you want all my needs to be met, and you cannot fail in meeting them.[16] I praise you for the wonderful realization that you do fulfill all your promises in my life.[17]

Thank you for your Word which will never return to you void.[18] I claim the promises of your Word for me, my family, and our lives. I take my stand upon the solid promises of your Word, Father.[19]

Thank you for meeting my every need.

References: *(1) Lamentations 3:23; (2) Philippians 4:19; (3) Psalms 25:6; (4) Hebrews 6:12; (5) Hebrews 11:6; (6) Philippians 1:6; (7) Matthew 6:33; (8) Matthew 6:8; (9) Psalms 37:4; (10) Lamentation 3:23; (11) 1 Thessalonians 5:28; (12) Psalms 63:3; (13) Luke 11:3; (14) Ephesians 3:20; (15) 1 Peter 5:7; (16) Matthew 19:26; (17) 2 Corinthians 1:20; (18) Isaiah 55:11; (19) 2 Peter 1:4.*

8. Thankfulness

Key Scripture: *"I will praise the name of God with a song, and will magnify him with thanksgiving"* (Ps. 69:30).

Key Thought: The attitude of gratitude leads to a happy life.

Prayer: Lord God, I praise you and adore you. You alone are worthy of praise, for you are the Creator of all things.[1] In you all things hold together.[2] Thank you, Lord, for who you are.

I will sing unto you; I will sing praises to you, because you are my Lord God.[3] In trust and obedience I praise your name. I praise you, Lord, according to your righteousness; I will sing praises to your name, O Lord Most High.[4]

Through your grace, I will praise your name forever. When I offer praise to you, Lord, I know I am glorifying you,[5] and I know this brings us both great joy and blessing. Let my mouth be filled with your praise and honor all day long, Father.[6]

I will sing of your mercies forever. With my mouth will I make known your faithfulness to all generations.[7] It is such a good thing to give thanks unto you, O Lord, and to sing praises unto your name. I want always to show forth your lovingkindness in the morning and your faithfulness every night.[8]

Because of who you are, and all you've done for me, I am able to offer the sacrifice of praise to you continually, and it is my desire to do so. It pleases me, Lord, to be able to give you the fruit of my lips, even praise to your name.[9]

Thank you, God, for everything.

References: *(1) John 1:3; (2) Colossians 1:17; (3) Judges 5:3; (4) Psalms 7:17; (5) Psalms 50:23; (6) Psalms 71:8; (7) Psalms 89:1; (8) Psalms 92:1-2; (9) Hebrews 13:15.*

9. Worry About Future Finances

Key Scripture: *"And we know that all things work together for good to them that love God, to them who are the called according to his purpose"* (Rom. 8:28).

Key Thought: You know who holds the future.

Prayer: Heavenly Father, because I know you care for me I also know that I can cast all my cares upon you. Forgive me for worrying; I cast all my cares upon you now, this moment.[1] I know I don't have to bear my burdens alone. Thank you for inviting me to come unto you and for your wonderful promise of rest.[2] I receive your rest as I lay my burdens of worry down.

When I look at my life, and at my finances, as I know I should (in the light of your Word), I realize I have no reason for worry whatsoever. Nothing shall be able to separate me from your love which is in Christ Jesus, my Lord — not things past nor present, nor things in the future.[3] Thank you, Father, for reassuring me that you are working your purposes out in my life and that you are the Master of all circumstances. I believe your promise which tells me that you will supply all my needs.[4]

There is no fear of the future to be found in your great love for me, because your perfect love casts out all fear.[5] You have told me, Father, not to fear because it is your good pleasure to give me the Kingdom.[6] I resolve never to lose sight of the precious promises of your glorious Word.

Lord, your command is not to worry about anything. Instead, you want me to spend my time in prayer and supplication, and to let my requests be known unto you, with thanksgiving.[7] How thankful I am that you have provided prayer and praise as practical outlets to prevent me from ever having to worry.

Concerning my finances, Lord, I will place my complete trust in you. I will not worry about tomorrow, because I know you will take care of all my tomorrows. With your help, I will take one day at a time, planning well, believing your Word, and receiving your promises.[8]

Thank you, Father, for the wonderful sense of security you are imparting to me.

References: *(1) 1 Peter 5:7; (2) Matthew 11:28; (3) Romans 8:38-39; (4) Philippians 4:19; (5) 1 John 4:18; (6) Luke 12:32; (7) Philippians 4:6-7; (8) Matthew 6:34.*

Books of Interest From
Victory House Publishers

PRAYERS THAT PREVAIL
(The Believer's Manual of Prayers)

PRAYERS THAT PREVAIL FOR YOUR CHILDREN

(A Parent's & Grandparent's Manual of Prayers)

PRAYING BIBLE PROMISES

BELIEVERS' PRAYERS AND PROMISES

BIBLE PRAYERS FOR ALL YOUR NEEDS

BREAKTHROUGH PRAYERS FOR WOMEN

PRAYER KEYS

KNOWING GOD INTIMATELY

HEALING PRAYERS

LETTERS FROM THE HEART OF GOD

PRAYING THE PSALMS

PRAYERS FOR OTHERS

TODAY GOD SAYS *(Devotional)*

IN THE SECRET PLACE WITH GOD